The Mindful Workplace

Developing Resilient Individuals and Resonant Organizations with MBSR

Michael Chaskalson

WILEY-BLACKWELL

A John Wiley & Sons, Ltd., Publication

This edition first published 2011
© 2011 John Wiley & Sons, Ltd.

Wiley-Blackwell is an imprint of John Wiley & Sons, formed by the merger of Wiley's global Scientific, Technical and Medical business with Blackwell Publishing.

Registered Office
John Wiley & Sons Ltd, The Atrium, Southern Gate, Chichester, West Sussex, PO19 8SQ, UK

Editorial Offices
The Atrium, Southern Gate, Chichester, West Sussex, PO19 8SQ, UK
350 Main Street, Malden, MA 02148-5020, USA
9600 Garsington Road, Oxford, OX4 2DQ, UK

For details of our global editorial offices, for customer services, and for information about how to apply for permission to reuse the copyright material in this book please see our website at www.wiley.com/wiley-blackwell.

Library of Congress Cataloging-in-Publication Data

Chaskalson, Michael.
   The mindful workplace : developing resilient individuals and resonant organizations with MBSR / Michael Chaskalson.
      p. cm.
   Includes index.
   ISBN 978-0-470-66158-1 (cloth) – ISBN 978-0-470-66159-8 (pbk.)
   1. Meditation–Therapeutic use.   2. Mindfulness-based cognitive therapy.   3. Stress management.   4. Job stress–Prevention.   I. Title.
   RC489.M55C43 2011
   615.8'52–dc22
                                                          2011009383

A catalogue record for this book is available from the British Library.

This book is published in the following electronic formats: ePDFs 9781119976981; Wiley Online Library 9781119976974; ePub 9781119976912

Set in Palatino 11.5/14.5 pt by Toppan Best-set Premedia Limited
Printed in Singapore by Ho Printing Singapore Pte Ltd

3   2012

To John Teasdale, Becca Crane and Ciaran Saunders (Ruchiraketu) for all the stimulating conversations on mindfulness and related themes. And to Annette (Dhirangama) for her love, kindness and constant support.

Thanks to Darren Reed, my editor at Wiley-Blackwell, for proposing this book and for steering it through the processes of publication with consummate grace. And to Leah Morin, for her wonderfully tactful, accurate and kindly copy-editing. It's been a delight to work with them both.

Contents

Contents

Foreword

We are entering a world of work where the combination of ever increasing globalization and technological advances are breaking our work up into ever smaller fragments. Faced with a continuous barrage of emails, constantly ringing phones, ever more demanding Twitter feeds and insistent Facebook updates, it's easy to let the instant, the pressing and the immediate overwhelm the important and the longer term. We are becoming overwhelmed by the sheer size of connectivity: over five billion people will soon potentially be connected to each other.

It's no surprise that, for many of us, three minutes is about as long as we can concentrate before being interrupted, and our relationships are becoming increasingly virtual and alienated. The results can be devastating. Skills become denuded as less time is spent in precious concentration, anxiety rises as the immediate overwhelms any sense of boundaries between us and our work, and loneliness becomes the central motif of much of our working lives. Faced with the sheer volume of stimulation, we are living our working lives on automatic pilot.

Yet, faced with the challenge of fragmentation and loneliness, what we need is not yet more careful time-management skills to eke out every last second; it is not the future promise of cognitive assistants capable of managing our inboxes; it is not even another programme to network and influence people. No: what we need is a way of thinking more mindfully about ourselves, our work and our companies. This message of mindfulness becomes ever more insistent when we consider the potential joy that longevity will bring to our working lives. The 50 years that many of us can expect to work could be a period of great meaning and satisfaction. But it also has the possibility of simply elongating what is already an energy-draining activity. Our working lives are rapidly shifting from a race to a marathon. Burnout for peak performance may have worked for a race – but it does not provide the resilience that a marathon takes.

The forces of technology, globalization, connectivity and demography together are creating an increasingly urgent need to shift the way we think about work and the skills and competencies we develop to build resilience. These mindful habits, skills and techniques will be crucial to navigating the road ahead.

It is these habits of mindfulness, the skills of self-awareness and the practices of meditation that Michael describes with so much wisdom and clarity. When we understand ourselves more profoundly, accept ourselves more fully and give ourselves an opportunity to reflect, then we build resilience for the path ahead.

The simplicity of Michael's message is underpinned by profound thought, insight and wisdom. Resilient lives are not made from grand gestures and the construction of grandiose theories. Resilience is built through the everyday, every-minute habits and exercises that punctuate our daily lives. When we consciously and mindfully choose to change the way we work and live, and consciously and mindfully build the habits of meaning into our lives, then we have the chance – the promise – of working with the forces that will shape our lives, rather than working against them.

Lynda Gratton
Professor of Management Practice
London Business School
Author of *The Shift: The Future of Work Is Already Here*

Preface

Mindfulness is a way of paying attention, in the present moment, to yourself, others and the world around you. It is a skill that you can train in, using techniques like meditation and yoga. As we'll see, research shows that people who do that are more aware of their thoughts and feelings and better able to manage them. Mindfulness training boosts your attention and concentration, raises your level of emotional intelligence, increases your resilience and improves your relationships.

This book makes the case for mindfulness training in the workplace. Put simply, its hypothesis is that people who are better at working with their minds and mental states will be more productive than those who are less skilled in these areas. Based on the emerging research evidence around the value of mindfulness training, the book discusses the relevance of that research to the world of work. It also tells the story of how mindfulness emerged from the Buddhist monasteries in which it was cloistered for 2500 years and is now being adopted as a mainstream health-care intervention.

Recommended as a frontline treatment by the UK National Institute for Health and Clinical Excellence (NICE), mindfulness is now also being used as a means of increasing resilience and enhancing emotional intelligence and overall effectiveness in a wide range of organizations: banks, media companies, industry, law and accountancy firms, the police, government and the military.

When I first began to practise mindfulness and meditation in 1975, sitting in patched jeans in draughty meditation rooms with my scruffy, enthusiastic companions, I never dreamed that I'd one day be wearing a suit and teaching it in corporate meeting rooms to senior partners in a global law firm. Nor could I ever have imagined that an organization like the US Marine Corps would adopt mindfulness training. But they have. A study conducted in the Corps found mindfulness training to be an effective means of helping combatants resist the various functional impairments associated with high-stress challenges. Marines who completed an eight-week Mindfulness-Based Stress Reduction (MBSR) course showed raised levels of cognitive control, increased self-awareness, more situational awareness and improved emotional regulation.

Studies like that were unthinkable in 1975. At best, it was a kind of fantasy. Wouldn't it be wonderful, my companions and I dreamed, if society at large could share in the benefits we were finding in our own mindfulness practice?

There are two key factors that seem to be driving the wider adoption of mindfulness. The first is its secularization. Thanks largely to the pioneering efforts of Jon Kabat-Zinn and his colleagues at the University of Massachusetts Medical School (of whom more later), mindfulness, which for thousands of years had been preserved almost exclusively in Buddhist contexts, is increasingly being offered as a purely secular form of mental training. Today you don't have to be a Buddhist to practise it and it is freely available to people from any religious background and to those with none.

Then, there is the science. When I first began to study mindfulness academically around 2003, there were a handful of respectable academic papers to refer to. Most of us in the field had read these and could refer to them easily. Now, that is impossible. There are thousands of papers out there and the volume of publications is increasing exponentially. From what we now know, based on published studies, mindfulness appears to be effective in reducing levels of stress and increasing levels of resilience and emotional intelligence. It raises the level of self-awareness and awareness of others; it increases interpersonal sensitivity and communication skills. It lowers rates of health-related absenteeism, leads to increased concentration and extends one's attention span. It reduces impulsivity and improves one's capacity to hold and manipulate information. It lowers levels of psychological distress and raises levels of well-being and overall work and life satisfaction. More and more of this kind of evidence is coming out each month.

But perhaps the most dramatic illustrations of the beneficial changes brought about by mindfulness training come from the field of neuroscience. Taking just one example, a study recently published[1] investigated pre- and post-changes in brain grey-matter concentration attributable to participation in an MBSR programme. It showed that after just eight weeks of mindfulness training there were significant increases in grey-matter concentration in brain regions involved in learning and memory processes, emotion regulation, self-referential processing and perspective-taking.

Evidence showing the clear benefits of mindfulness training increases every day and the uptake of mindfulness practices across the board in our culture is growing steadily. This book aims to show the relevance of this evidence and this training to today's rapidly changing, uncertain and often stressful workplace. I hope it will play its own small part in helping to make these remarkable techniques more widely available.

Reference

1   Hölzel, B.K., Carmody, J., Vangel, M., *et al.* (2011) Mindfulness practice leads to increases in regional brain gray matter density. *Psychiatry Research: Neuroimaging*, 191 (1), 36–43.

Introduction
The Business Case for Mindfulness Training

In a conference room on the edge of London 15 employees of one of the world's largest online retailers sit in a circle. The room is normally used for PowerPoint presentations of strategy options or market-research data, but today is different. One of the company's legal counsellors is here, as are the managers of various divisions. There are strategists present, HR people and a small cluster of people concerned with new-business development. It's not been an easy time for the firm. They have had their world more or less to themselves for almost a decade, but rival companies have recently been eating away at their market share. A series of high-profile litigation cases have begun to affect crucial public perceptions of a company once thought of as hip, radical and somehow friendly. Some think their approach is beginning to look a

The Mindful Workplace: Developing Resilient Individuals and Resonant Organizations with MBSR, First Edition. M. Chaskalson.
© 2011 John Wiley & Sons, Ltd. Published 2011 by John Wiley & Sons, Ltd.

little tired. And the market is beginning to turn – it seems we may be on the brink of a deep recession.

It is the final session of an eight-week mindfulness course that the company has laid on for anyone who wants to attend. The participants are discussing what they have learned: 'It's been life-changing for me', the legal counsellor tells the group.

> You all know what's been going on in my corner of this world these past weeks. The stress levels have been immense but the work we've been doing in the mindfulness group has made such a difference. Not just at work . . . I've been, I guess, somehow more *human* at home too. Not so snappy, more available. Of course it's impossible to evaluate how I'd have been if I'd not done it, but my sense is that I've been sharper, more creative, and certainly less difficult to be around.

It's not been easy for the group to follow this programme. Among other things, it has involved a daily meditation practice of 20 minutes or more at a stretch. Some participants were new to meditation and all of them have very full lives. Their work, family and social lives make huge demands on their time and, prior to the course, their minds were constantly and very actively preoccupied. Just fitting in the taught, group-based part of the course for two hours a week over eight weeks was a challenge, to say nothing of the home-practice requirement. Yet attendance on the course was voluntary and each person had a sense, from the introductory taster session they attended, that there were real benefits on offer. Having persisted with the programme they are now reporting the benefits.

The Mindfulness-Based Stress Reduction (MBSR) programme they have been attending has its origins at the Stress

Reduction Clinic that was founded by Dr Jon Kabat-Zinn and his colleagues at the University of Massachusetts Medical School in 1979. The term 'mindfulness' points to an idea or approach that is said to have first been described by the Buddha over 2500 years ago. It is a form of sustained present-moment awareness – of yourself, others and the world around you. The UK Mental Health Foundation's 2010 *Mindfulness Report* describes mindfulness in the clinical context as:

> an integrative, mind-body based approach that helps people change the way they think and feel about their experiences, especially stressful experiences. It involves paying attention to our thoughts and feelings so we become more aware of them, less enmeshed in them, and better able to manage them.[1] (p. 6)

Since its inception, the eight-week MBSR programme that Kabat-Zinn and his colleagues developed – as well as variants upon it – has been subject to considerable research. There have been thousands of peer-reviewed papers[i] published that speak of its effectiveness in a wide variety of applications. Comparative studies of some of the primary peer-reviewed empirical literature about the course have judged the programme and its variants to be effective.[2–4] Based on a review of this literature, the Mental Health Foundation's report suggests that evidence coming from mindfulness and well-being research shows that mindfulness confers significant benefits on health, well-being and quality of life in general. Each of the benefits that the report draws attention to has significant implications for people's performance in the workplace – either in terms of their levels of stress and productivity or in terms of the qualities of their interpersonal relationships, as leaders or team members. According to the report:

- People who are more mindful are less likely to experience psychological distress, including depression and anxiety. They are less neurotic, more extroverted and report greater well-being and life satisfaction.
- People who are more mindful have greater awareness, understanding and acceptance of their emotions, and recover from bad moods more quickly.
- People who are more mindful have less frequent negative thoughts and are more able to let them go when they arise.
- People who are more mindful have higher, more stable self-esteem that is less dependent on external factors.
- People who are more mindful enjoy more satisfying relationships, are better at communicating and are less troubled by relationship conflict, as well as less likely to think negatively of their partners as a result of conflict.
- Mindfulness is correlated with emotional intelligence, which itself has been associated with good social skills, ability to cooperate and ability to see another person's perspective.
- People who are mindful are also less likely to react defensively or aggressively when they feel threatened. Mindfulness seems to increase self-awareness, and is associated with greater vitality.
- Being more mindful is linked with higher success in reaching academic and personal goals.
- Practising meditation has repeatedly been shown to improve people's attention, as well as improve job performance, productivity and satisfaction, and to enable better relationships with colleagues, resulting in a reduction of work-related stress.
- People who are mindful feel more in control of their behaviour and are more able to override or change internal thoughts and feelings and resist acting on impulse.

- Meditation practices more generally have been shown to increase blood flow, reduce blood pressure and protect people at risk of developing hypertension; they have also been shown to reduce the risk of developing and dying from cardiovascular disease, and to reduce the severity of cardiovascular disease when it does arise.
- People who meditate have fewer hospital admissions for heart disease, cancer and infectious diseases, and visit their doctor half as often as people who don't meditate.
- Mindfulness can reduce addictive behaviour, and meditation practices generally have been found to help reduce use of illegal drugs, prescribed medication, alcohol and caffeine.[1]

This list alone might stand as a good case for the introduction of workplace mindfulness training. The case extends well beyond this, however, as later chapters will show. For now, it is worth just touching on the issue of stress and its costs. As we will see, mindfulness training enhances interpersonal relationships, it develops emotional intelligence, increases resilience, enhances innovation and creativity, and extends one's attention span. All of these have significant workplace benefits. But it is as a stress-reduction intervention that mindfulness training has so far been most widely known.

In the United Kingdom, stress in the workplace is running at epidemic levels. The Labour Force Survey conducted by the UK Office for National Statistics in 2007/2008 estimated that 442 000 individuals in Britain who worked in the last year believed that they were experiencing work-related stress at a level that was making them ill.[5] Around 13.6% of all working individuals in the United Kingdom in 2007 thought their job was very or extremely stressful.[6] An estimated 237 000 people who worked in 2007/2008 became aware of work-related stress, depression or anxiety, giving an annual incidence rate of 780 cases per 100000 workers; in the same year, stress, depression and anxiety accounted for an estimated 13.5 million lost working days.[5] Commenting on the cost of stress to business, Ben Wilmott, employee-relations adviser at the UK Chartered Institute of Personnel Development, estimates that the direct and indirect costs of employee absence to UK businesses is around £1800 per employee per year.[7] There is a powerful economic case for helping individuals deal with stress.

In a study carried out with 141 employees of West Virginia University[8] between 1994 and 1996 – 44% of whom perceived themselves to be in a constant state of high stress prior to the programme – participants reported a 31% decrease in the mean number of medical symptoms, a 17% decrease in the mean impact of daily hassles and a 30.7% decrease in psychological distress. These improvements were actually greater at the three-month follow-up. Participants showed significant improvement in all 21 categories on the stress-map inventory that was used in the study and reported a number of positive changes in their attitudes and behaviour as a result of participating in the programme. By the end of the pro-gramme 92% of them were still meditating.

A mindfulness-based programme offered to workers at Transport for London resulted in major changes to the level of health-related absenteeism. Days taken off due to stress, depression and anxiety fell by over 70% in the following three years (absences for all health conditions were halved). Those who took the course also reported significant improvements in their quality of life – 80% said their relationships had improved, 79% said they were more able to relax and 53% said they were happier in their jobs.[1]

In another MBSR workplace study,[9] carried out with 48 employees of a biotech company in Madison, Wisconsin, subjects were evaluated for brain and immune function. These were compared with a wait-list control group. At the end of the programme those who had participated in the MBSR course had significantly greater activation in their brain's left prefrontal cortex (LPFC). LPFC activation – as we shall see in more detail in a later chapter – corresponds to more 'positive' emotional processing and is thought to reflect more adaptive responses to stress. The MBSR group also showed a stronger antibody response to a flu vaccine when compared with the control group, and the magnitude of this was positively associated with the increased LPFC activation. The broader significance of these changes, and their implications for issues such as interpersonal relationships, creativity and innovation, will be discussed in more detail in a later chapter. For now, though, it is worth noting their impact on levels of stress. As marked by the changes in question, participants began the course with higher stress levels and completed it with their stress levels reduced.

Depression is another public-health matter with cost implications for the workplace. A study carried out in the United States, for example, suggests that the per-capita annual cost of depression is significantly more than that of hypertension or back problems and is comparable to that of diabetes or heart disease.[10] People with depression also have more sick days than people suffering from other conditions,[11] and depression in the major industrial countries is running at epidemic levels. At any one time, 10% of people have experienced clinical depression in the past year, and between 20 and 25% of women and 7 and 12% of men will suffer from it at some point in their lives. People who have experienced two or more major episodes of depression have a greater than 70% risk of depressive relapse.[12]

The good news is that mindfulness training can make a huge difference. The National Institute for Health and Clinical Excellence (NICE), the body that recommends treatment practices to the NHS, recommends an eight-week course in mindfulness as a front-line treatment for relapsing depression.[13] The basis of this recommendation is the accumulated evidence from four large-scale randomised control trials. The last of these, conducted by Kuyken and colleagues in 2008[14] showed that an eight-week mindfulness-training intervention – Mindfulness-Based Cognitive Therapy (MBCT), which is based upon, and is very similar in its content to, Kabat-Zinn's MBSR programme – was more effective than maintenance doses of anti-depressants in helping people stay well after significant depression. So in relation to stress and to depression, which are often related conditions, mindfulness training can have a significant impact, and there is a strong economic case that could be made for the use of such training in maintaining workplace health.

The benefits of mindfulness training, however, as we will see, extend far beyond the domain of occupational health. Richard Boyatzis, professor of organizational behaviour at the Weatherhead School of Management, speaks of mindfulness as 'the capacity to be fully aware of all that one experiences *inside the self* – body, mind, heart, spirit – and to pay full attention to what is happening *around us* – people, the natural world, our surroundings and events' (original emphasis).[15] For Boyatzis, mindfulness is a key management competency. Mindfulness, he says, starts with self-awareness. This self-knowledge enables you to choose how best to respond to people and situations. It allows you to be consistent, presenting yourself simply as you are. We trust – and follow –

people who are authentic and whose behaviour, beliefs and values are aligned: people whom we do not have to constantly second-guess. Mindfulness skills, he says, enable us to make better choices because we can recognize and deal with our own thoughts, feelings and physical sensations. This helps us to make better sense of people and of the situations around us. Our perceptions are then clearer, less clouded by our usual filters and biases. Through the purposeful, conscious direction of our attention, we see things that would normally pass us by and gain access to deeper insight and wisdom. As a result, we make better choices.[16] This all makes for more effective management. It also makes for more effective teams.

Boyatzis and McKee[15] coined the term 'resonant leadership' to describe the way in which great leaders attune to their people and draw out and amplify what is best in them. The same can be said of teams. A resonant team is one whose members are *attuned* to each other, cooperative and mutually supportive. A dissonant team, by contrast, is inharmonious. The neural integration that mindfulness training brings about[17 (p. 290)] can significantly increase our capacity for attunement. Mindfulness makes for more effective teams and leaders.

Enabling us to become more aware of ourselves, others and the world around us, mindfulness training helps us to deal more effectively with issues of stress. It also enables us better to handle the welter of information and complexity that marks our working lives.

Participants in mindfulness courses learn to work more consciously and effectively with their minds and mental states. This is a form of training that we all ought to have learned in school (and it is a wonderful fact that, in places like the United Kingdom, there are projects afoot to bring mindfulness training to school pupils).[ii] It is never too late to learn these skills, however, and workplace organizations have a key role to play.

As I hope this book will show, a more mindful workplace should experience higher overall levels of employee well-being and resilience. Characteristics of such a workplace would be:

- lower levels of stress and illness-related absenteeism;
- more employee engagement;
- greater productivity;
- less conflict;
- higher levels of job satisfaction;
- lower levels of employee turnover;
- higher levels of creativity and innovation.

All in all, given the relatively low cost of mounting such trainings, the potential return on investment is considerable.

Notes

i   See www.mindfulexperience.org for a list of current papers.
ii   See, for example, http://mindfulnessinschools.org/.

References

1   Mental Health Foundation (2010) Mindfulness Report, London. Executive summary available from http://www.bemindful.co.uk/media/downloads/Executive%20Summary.pdf (accessed 28 February 2011).
2   Grossman, P., Niemann, L., Schmidt, S., and Walach, H. (2004) Mindfulness-based stress reduction and health benefits: A meta-analysis. *Journal of Psychosomatic Research*, 57, 35–43.

3   Baer, R.A. (2003) Mindfulness training as a clinical intervention: A conceptual and empirical review. *Clinical Psychology: Science and Practice*, 10 (2), 125–143.

4   Chiesa, A., and Serretti, A. (2010) A systematic review of neurobiological and clinical features of mindfulness meditations. *Psychological Medicine*, 40, 1239–1252.

5   Health and Safety Executive (2007/2008) Stress-related and psychological disorders, http://www.hse.gov.uk/statistics/causdis/stress/ (accessed 28 February 2011).

6   Webster, S., Buckley, P., and Rose, I. (2007) Psychosocial working conditions in Britain in 2007, http://www.hse.gov.uk/statistics/pdf/pwc2007.pdf (accessed 3 March 2011).

7   Government Business (n.d.) The fine line between pressure and stress, http://www.governmentbusiness.co.uk/content/view/551/52/ (accessed 8 March 2011).

8   Williams, K. (2006) Mindfulness-Based Stress Reduction (MBSR) in a Worksite Wellness program, in *Mindfulness-Based Treatment Approaches: Clinician's Guide to Evidence Base and Applications* (ed. R.A. Baer), Academic Press, Burlington, MA, pp. 361–376.

9   Davidson, R.J., Kabat-Zinn, J., Schumacher, J., *et al.* (2003) Alterations in brain and immune function produced by mindfulness meditation. *Psychosomatic Medicine*, 65, 564–570.

10 Sullivan, J. (2005) Promoting health and productivity for depressed patients in the workplace. *Journal of Managed Care Pharmacy*, 11 (3), S12–15.

11 Druss, B.G., Rosenheck, R.A., and Sledge, W. (2000) Health and disability costs of depressive illness in a major U.S. corporation. *American Journal of Psychiatry*, 157 (8), 1274–1278.

12 Segal, Z.V., Williams, J.M.G., and Teasdale, J.D. (2002) *Mindfulness-Based Cognitive Therapy for Depression: A New Approach to Preventing Relapse*, Guilford Press, London.

13 NICE (2004) Depression: Management of Depression in Primary and Secondary Care. Clinical Guideline 23 (December).

14 Kuyken, W., Byford, S., Taylor, R.S., *et al.* (2008) Mindfulness-based cognitive therapy to prevent relapse in recurrent depression. *Journal of Consulting and Clinical Psychology*, 76, 966–978.

15 Boyatzis, R., and McKee, A. (2005) *Resonant Leadership*, Harvard Business School Press, Boston.

16 Boyatzis, R., and McKee, A. (2005) In a bad spot? Try mindfulness, http://hbswk.hbs.edu/archive/5069.html (accessed 3 March 2011).

17 Siegel, D.J. (2007) *The Mindful Brain: Reflection and Attunement in the Cultivation of Well-Being*, W.W. Norton & Company, New York.

1

What Is Mindfulness?

It's hard to define exactly what we mean by mindfulness – it's more like a rainbow than a single colour. Kabat-Zinn speaks of it as a way of paying attention: on purpose, in the present moment and non-judgementally[1 (p. 4)] to whatever arises in the field of your experience, and that is a good starting point. Mindfulness is a way of paying attention 'on purpose'. When you're mindful, you know that you're mindful. You're aware of what you're thinking, what you're feeling and what you're sensing in your body, and you know that you're aware of these things. Much of the time we're just not aware in that sense.

Take the case of James, who is driving to an important meeting for which he's late. He's feeling tense, hassled and not particularly mindful. A long line of cars has already built

The Mindful Workplace: Developing Resilient Individuals and Resonant Organizations with MBSR, First Edition. M. Chaskalson.

up as he approaches the traffic lights on a busy junction. Just as the line begins to close up at the red signal, another car races up from behind him, squeezes past at the last moment and takes James's place in the queue. James is now precisely one car's length further back from the lights than he would have been had that car not pushed in. In fact, he's about 4.2 metres further back and, at an average urban speed of around 15 miles per hour (40.234 metres per second), that means he'll be more or less one tenth of a second later for his meeting.

But it doesn't feel like that to James. In that moment, from his perspective, it feels like a complete disaster. 'Now I'm going to be *really* late. People are so rude, so pushy! Oh . . . !!!' His shoulders tighten, his hands clench on the wheel and his mind begins to race. 'What a mess! How could I be so late? They'll never take me seriously. This is *so* unprofessional . . . I *hate* being late . . . What a pig – pushing in front like that . . . ' His stomach starts to churn and he can feel heartburn coming on. His whole body starts to tighten up and he begins to sweat. What James is actually doing here is setting up the conditions for a not very successful meeting. He's going to be in pretty poor shape when he walks into the meeting room a few minutes late (and one tenth of a second later than he would have been had that car not pushed in front).

Had James been paying mindful attention to his experience, had he been even a little mindful at any point in that unfolding scenario, things might have gone quite differently. He might, for example, have become aware of the way he was gripping the steering wheel. He might have found, for instance, that it was almost painful and that the tension spread from there up his arms and into his shoulders. Bringing some mindful attention to that, he could have deliberately loosened his grip on the wheel. His shoulders might then have softened and his stomach begun to settle. Taking a few deep breaths, he might have thought, 'Ah well, one car in front – that won't hurt too much. Now, how shall I best handle this? Will I apologize for being late or just carry on regardless?'

Or he might have become aware of how he was feeling. 'Gosh I'm angry! Wow! My stomach's really churning . . . like a washing machine! OK – let's just chill a bit. A few deep breaths . . . ' Or he might have become aware of his thoughts. 'Oh yes . . . Here I go again. Catastrophizing. I'm a few minutes late and I write off the whole meeting . . . OK . . . Time for a few deep breaths . . . Now how am I going to handle this meeting? What would be my most effective opening . . . ?' With some mindfulness training, James might have learned to bring a different quality of awareness to his thoughts, feelings or body sensations at times of distress. This capacity to know what we're thinking, feeling or sensing as it is going on is what we might call the 'metacognitive' dimension of mindfulness.

Metacognition refers to our knowledge about our own cognitive processes or anything related to them.[2] In the context of mindfulness, metacognition extends into the domains of feelings and body-sensations as well. All of these – thoughts, feelings and body-sensations – are experienced in the mind, and metacognition is the mind aware *that* it is thinking, *that* it is feeling, *that* it is sensing. Any one of these metacognitive elements of mindfulness can enter our experience at any time and transform it. Had James become aware that he was feeling a pain in his hands and shoulders from gripping the wheel, or that he was angry, or that he was catastrophizing, he would have begun to have a choice around where things might go next. He would have been able to make wiser choices, and one of the purposes of mindfulness practice is to significantly increase the chance of that happening. Had James been in a position to deploy any one of the metacognitive skills as the car pushed in front of him at the traffic lights, his meeting would have been far more effective – and more profitable for his firm.

Another quality of mindful attention, according to Kabat-Zinn's definition, is that it is rooted 'in the present moment'. So often our attention is oriented towards the future or the past. Imagine the case of Emily, walking from the Tube station to her office on a sunny spring morning. She's completely oblivious to the sensation of the first rays of early summer sun on her face. Nor does she catch the fresh fragrance of a shrub she passes that has just burst into flower. The sense of vitality and well-being that might have come from either of these experiences is lost to her. Instead she's fixated on her to-do list for the next week. Not that she needs to be – she could recite it by heart. She's been over it again and again and again ever since she woke up, but there she goes again, rehearsing the tasks ahead of her.

Emily thinks of herself as conscientious. She's a good worker, focused on her job. But the way she's needlessly and unproductively rehearsing her to-do list – checking its details maybe for the hundredth time that morning – keeps her from refreshing herself in simple ways. She'll arrive at work in good time and get on with her tasks efficiently, but her performance won't be quite as good as it might have been. Preoccupied with her to-do list, she's lost some really useful opportunities to refresh herself and to broaden her mental and emotional horizons. But more than that. Preoccupied with her to-do list, or with her attention wandering into the past or future, Emily isn't as present and wholehearted in her approach to her work as she thinks she is.

Sometimes her attention wanders into the past: 'That meeting last week . . . If only I'd taken the chance to make that point, and if only Will hadn't spoken in that way, and maybe it would have been better if I'd worn those other shoes . . . ' Or it drifts into the future: 'What will I make for dinner tonight? And should we book that holiday before prices rise again, and what will I wear tomorrow . . . ?' And so Emily's attention runs. She thinks she's diligently getting on with her tasks but some of the time it's as if she's put her mind onto a kind of 'automatic pilot' and let it just run on as it does.

Maybe you've had the experience of driving 30 miles down the road and then suddenly coming to – 'Oh gosh, we're here already. How did I do that? I've been miles away . . . ' You were thinking, or planning, or dreaming and you were simply driving on automatic pilot, performing quite complex tasks – changing gears, judging distances, braking, indicating – without any conscious awareness that you were doing them. It seems to work. And because it seems to work we put more and more of our lives onto automatic pilot.

When we were really young each moment was fresh and new and we were right there for each experience. But as we grow older it all starts to feel completely familiar and we begin to do more and more of it automatically and that seems to be OK. But is it? With our attention set on automatic pilot we miss things. Certainly, we miss the well-being elements that we might get from noticing the first blossoms of spring or the vibrant shades of the autumn leaves. But there are other things that we might miss as well. That particular tone in your child's greeting in the morning that says he's being bullied at school and somehow can't talk about it right now. But you miss it, because you're just doing family breakfast on automatic pilot. Or that flicker of expression on a colleague's face that says that there's something important going on at home that she really needs to talk about. Or that glance in a client's eye that might have opened a whole new dimension to the negotiation.

On automatic pilot we miss things, and some of what we miss might have a significant impact on our performance at work. But more than that: at the deepest level, as Kabat-Zinn has pointed out,[3] if life is just one moment of experience, followed by another moment of experience, followed by another moment of experience, and then another, and another . . . and then you're dead, well, wouldn't it be good to show up for some of those experiences? To show up for your life – while you still have it? To pay attention – in the present moment? The capacity to come out of automatic pilot a bit more often, to place your attention where you want it to be and to keep it there for longer is a known outcome of mindfulness training.[4]

One of the really intriguing studies on the relationship between mindfulness training and attentional effectiveness was carried out by Jha and Stanley with a group of US Marines.[5] Their findings featured in *Joint Force Quarterly*, the advisory journal of the Joint Chiefs of Staff. A group of 31 Marines about to be deployed to Iraq and undergoing 'stress-inoculation' training, which helps habituate them to the extreme mental rigours of combat, received an eight-week mindfulness course (a control group of 17 did not receive the course). Jha and Stanley then measured the protective influence of the mindfulness training on the Marines' working memory. Her findings suggested that, just as daily physical exercise leads to physical fitness, engaging in mindfulness exercises on a regular basis improved the Marines' 'mind-fitness' by extending their working memory under stress. That, she claims,[6] safeguards them against distraction and emotional reactivity and lets them maintain a mental workspace that ensures quick and considered decisions and action plans. Besides offering some protection to combatants from post-traumatic stress and other anxiety disorders, the mindfulness training enhanced the clarity of thinking needed for soldiers fighting in challenging and ambiguous counter-insurgency zones.

For Jha, this study showed that mindfulness training might help anyone who must maintain peak performance in the face of extremely stressful circumstances: the emergency services, relief workers, trauma surgeons, professional and Olympic athletes and so on. But actually very few people in the workplace are immune from periods of extreme demand these days and it's hard to imagine anyone whose work and productivity would not benefit from an increased capacity to deploy their attention in ways that their tasks require.

The last quality of mindful awareness that Kabat-Zinn draws attention to is that it is 'non-judgemental'. This doesn't mean that if you are mindful you don't make judgements or that you give up the powers of discrimination. Far from it. But it does involve dropping a certain kind of judgemental-ism, especially the tendency constantly to judge ourselves in a critical light. Many of us have a habit of judging ourselves that disguises itself as an attempt to help us lead better lives and be better people. But actually it's a kind of irrational tyranny that can never be satisfied.[7] The mindful approach, by contrast, is to let yourself experience what you're experiencing without censoring it, without blocking things out or constantly wishing they were other than they are. Mindfulness training encourages us to bring an attitude of warm, kindly curiosity to whatever we experience – in thoughts, feelings and body-sensations – from moment to moment. It enables us to let what *is* the case *be* the case.

Imagine the case of Laura, who is based in the London office of her company and has been asked to present her team's findings to a group of senior people in New York by video link. She hates doing that. Standing alone in the video suite, facing an inert camera and being seen by a number of people whose names she barely knows, 3500 miles away. It makes her nervous. But Laura thinks she ought not to feel nervous. It's just a camera, after all. She's done video-link presentations before. 'It's so stupid being nervous', she thinks, adding an additional layer of harsh, self-critical judgement onto an already difficult experience.

When the video-link goes live Laura is suddenly overcome with nerves. Her face flushes and, trying to suppress the flush, she freezes and fluffs her opening lines. Struggling to catch up with herself she stumbles again and again. At the end, after a less than satisfactory videoconference, she dashes for the lavatory and bursts into tears. 'I'm just rubbish', she tells herself. 'I can't do this job. I'm just no good – I'm not up to it . . . ' None of that is true and Laura stays in her position, but her confidence has been seriously undermined and it takes her weeks to recover.

With a little mindfulness training it might have gone differently. Taking a more mindful, more accepting approach to her feelings and sensations, Laura might have noticed the feeling of butterflies in her stomach. 'I'm a bit nervous about this', she might have thought, and taken a few moments simply to acknowledge what was going on for her – that tightness in her jaw, the tension at her shoulders. Exploring these sensations and investigating her feelings with an attitude of kindly curiosity, she might have said to herself: 'OK – I'm nervous. I can be with that. I'll just do the best I can with this.' Planting her feet firmly on the floor of the video suite, rooted and upright, accepting herself as she actually found herself, a deeper confidence might have emerged and the videoconference might have been quite different.

Learning to pay attention in this way – on purpose, in the present moment and non-judgementally – participants in mindfulness courses begin to experience a fundamental shift in perspective. They learn to dis-identify from the contents of their consciousness – their thoughts, feelings and body sensations – and to view their moment-by-moment experience with greater clarity and objectivity.

This capacity to shift perspective has been described as a form of *reperceiving*.[8] Rather than being immersed in the drama of their personal narratives or life stories, participants on MBSR courses learn the skill of standing back a little and witnessing what is going on for them. They learn that the phenomena that arise in practices such as meditation are distinct from the mind contemplating them.[9 (p. 146)] This skill of reperceiving brings about a subtle turning about in consciousness in which what was previously 'subject' now becomes 'object'.

Taking the example of Laura and her experience of the video presentation, before learning mindfulness she was simply nervous. You might say she was in a bit of a state. But she didn't acknowledge that to herself and it coloured her subjective experience quite dramatically. Had she been more mindful, she might have reperceived the experience. Some elements of her nervousness would then have become an objective experience she could attend to. Noticing the butterflies in her stomach, for example, she might have attended to that with warmth and curiosity. 'Wow, I'm a bit nervous. My stomach's really fluttering – gosh, it really *is* fluttering – so that's what they mean when they talk of "butterflies in the stomach" . . . What a strange feeling . . . ' That shift in perspective would have allowed her to enter the video suite in a very different mode of mind – an 'approach' mode of mind, characterized by warmth, acceptance and curiosity – and she would probably have handled the situation much more effectively. Had Laura been able to enjoy the benefits of a mindfulness course put on in her workplace, she and her company would both have experienced considerable benefit.

This capacity to reperceive, although it needs to be learned and is something we can consciously train in, is simply a continuation of the way we naturally develop. As we grow from infancy we develop an increasing capacity for objectivity about our internal experience. To illustrate this developmental process – one of increasing objectivity over time – Shapiro and colleagues describe how, on a mother's birthday, her eight-year-old son gives her flowers, while her three-year-old gives her his favourite toy. That is developmentally appropriate. The three-year-old is naturally caught in the limits of his perspective. For him, the world is still largely 'subjective'. It is an extension of his self and, as a result, he can't differentiate his own desires from those of his mother. As he develops, however, a shift in perspective occurs and there is an ever-increasing capacity to sense the perspective of others. He begins to see that his mother's needs and wishes are different from his own. What was previously subject – his identification with his mother – has become an object which he now realizes he is separate from. This is the dawning of empathy – the awareness of his mother as a separate person with her own needs and desires.[8] One aspect of our development from infancy to adulthood is an unconscious increase in our capacity to reperceive. We don't know that we're doing it, but as we grow we become more objective in certain respects. Mindfulness practice continues this natural process, but now at a conscious level. With mindfulness training we can begin consciously to develop an increasing capacity for objectivity with regard to our internal and external experience.[8]

This 'reperceiving' is not the same as detachment. It's not about distancing yourself from your experience to the point of apathy or numbness. Instead, the experience of mindful reperceiving gives rise to a deep knowing: a greater intimacy with whatever arises moment by moment. Mindfulness allows for a degree of distance from your experience in the sense that you become clearer about what it is you're experiencing. But this doesn't translate into a disconnection or dissociation. Instead, it allows you to experience the changing flow of your mental and physical experiences without identifying with them or clinging to them. Ultimately, this gives rise to a profound, penetrative, non-conceptual seeing into the nature of mind and world.[10] [(p. 146)] Rather than leading to a cold detachment, this lets you connect more intimately with your moment-to-moment experience, allowing it to rise and fall and change naturally, as it does. You begin to experience *what is* instead of a commentary or story *about* what is. Rather than creating apathy or indifference, this helps you to experience greater richness, texture and depth – from moment to moment. Shapiro and colleagues speak of this as a form of 'intimate detachment', and that captures both sides of the experience.[8]

The shift from unmindfulness to mindfulness – from unconsciously clinging to, or pushing away from, every moment of experience to the state of intimate objectivity around that experience – is almost alchemical in its subtlety. A kind of transmutation takes place that allows what was once threatening or compulsively desirable to become much more tolerable and effectively manageable, maybe even interesting and vital. But this shift *is* subtle. There are pitfalls and bear traps all along the way as people begin to take up mindfulness practice for themselves. The unwary can find themselves forcing their attention in an attempt to gain concentration, or alienating themselves from the natural flow of their emotions in an attempt to gain some objectivity. The tendency to impose another framework upon your existing pattern of experience when you first hear about mindfulness is quite natural. But mindfulness doesn't work like that. It can only arise as a product of mindfulness practice. It can't be imposed or plugged into an existing framework; for mindfulness practice to be effective it needs to be taught by an experienced mindfulness teacher.

As much as anything, mindfulness is caught – not taught. The lived, embodied experience of the mindfulness instructor, as witnessed by those he or she is teaching, is as much a source of learning as the techniques imparted. The instructor's tone of voice and mindful attention, their attitude of kindly acceptance and their openness to the enormous variety of their students' reported experience is a hugely important part of their teaching.

All the clinical trials that have shown mindfulness to be effective have been conducted on groups that have been led by trained, experienced mindfulness teachers. As the results of these trials filter out into the wider society and as mindfulness comes to be taken up more and more enthusiastically – especially in organizational environments – there is a real danger that inexperienced HR and Learning and Development personnel will be asked to lead groups based on their own very limited experience. The authors of *Mindfulness-Based Cognitive Therapy for Depression*[11] suggest that people leading mindfulness courses should have at least two years of formal daily mindfulness practice behind them. These days in the United Kingdom there are several good-quality mindfulness teacher-training programmes available[i] and there are valuable free-access resources, such as the 'Good Practice Guidance for Teaching Mindfulness-Based Courses'.[ii] Without adequately trained teachers, mindfulness courses might even be counterproductive.

With all of these caveats in mind, it is time to look at what we actually mean by mindfulness practice and that is the subject of the next chapter. Before then, though, we leave this chapter with a short meditation – an eating meditation. But we're not going to eat very much at all. In fact we'll eat just one raisin – mindfully.

Try this:

The Raisin Exercise

Get hold of a single raisin and find somewhere quiet where you can sit for 10 or 15 minutes and give your full attention to this exercise.

1. Holding
   - Let the raisin rest in your palm. Take a few moments to become aware of its weight.
   - Then, become aware of its temperature – any warmth or coolness it may have.
2. Looking
   - Give the raisin your full attention, really looking.
   - Become aware of the pattern of colour and shape that the raisin makes as it rests on your palm – almost like an abstract painting.
3. Touching
   - Aware of the sense of movement in your muscles as you do this, pick up the raisin between the thumb and forefinger of your other hand.

- Explore the outside texture of the raisin as you roll it very gently between your thumb and forefinger.
- Squeeze it ever so slightly and notice that this might give you a sense of its interior texture.
- Notice that you can feel this difference just with your thumb and forefinger – the *interior* texture and the *exterior* texture.

4. Seeing
   - Lift the raisin to a place where you can really focus on it and begin to examine it in much more detail.
   - See its highlights and shadows and how these change as it moves in the light.
   - Notice how facets of it appear and disappear – how it may seem to have ridges and valleys and how these may shift and change.

5. Smelling
   - Again aware of the sense of movement in your muscles, begin to move the raisin very slowly towards your mouth.
   - As it passes by your nose you may become aware of its fragrance. With each inhalation, really explore that fragrance.
   - Become aware of any changes that may be taking place now in your mouth or stomach – any salivation, perhaps.

6. Placing
   - Bring the raisin up to your lips. Explore the delicate sensation of touch here.
   - Now place it in your mouth and don't chew.

- Just let it rest on your tongue, noticing any very faint flavour that may be there.
- Feel the contact it makes with the roof of the mouth, perhaps.
- Now move it to between your back teeth and just let it rest there – again without chewing.
- Notice any urges or impulses in the body.

7. Tasting
   - Now take a single bite. Just one. Notice any flavour.
   - Then take another bite. Notice any change in flavour.
   - Then another bite, and another.

8. Chewing
   - Now slowly, very slowly, chew.
   - Be aware of sound, of texture, of flavour and of change.
   - Keep chewing in this way, very slowly, until there is almost nothing left to chew.

9. Swallowing
   - When there is almost nothing left to chew, swallow. See if you can be aware of the intention to swallow as it first arises.

10. Finishing
    - As best you can, follow what is left of the raisin as it moves down towards your stomach and you lose sight of it altogether.
    - How does your body feel now as you've completed that exercise?
    - What did you notice that you might not have been aware of before?

Notes

i   See Appendix 4.
ii See Appendix 1.

References

1   Kabat-Zinn, J. (1994) *Wherever You Go, There You Are: Mindfulness Meditation in Everyday Life*, Hyperion, New York.
2   Flavell, J.H. (1976) Metacognitive aspects of problem solving, in *The Nature of Intelligence* (ed. L.B. Resnick), Erlbaum, Hillsdale, NJ, p. 232.
3   Moyers, B. (1993) *Healing and the Mind*, Broadway Books, New York.
4   Jha, A.P., Krompinger, J., and Baime, M.J. (2007) Mindfulness training modifies subsystems of attention. *Cognitive, Affective, & Behavioral Neuroscience*, 7 (2), 109–119.
5   Jha, A.P., and Stanley, E.A. (2010) Examining the protective effects of mindfulness training on working memory capacity and affective experience. *Emotion*, 10 (1), 54–64.
6   Nichols, P. (2010) Semper Zen: Cognitive neuroscientist Amishi Jha studies mindfulness training for military preparedness, http://www.sas.upenn.edu/home/SASFrontiers/jha.html (accessed 3 March 2011).
7   Williams, M., Teasdale, J., Segal, S., and Kabat-Zinn, J. (2007) *The Mindful Way through Depression: Freeing Yourself from Chronic Unhappiness*, Guilford Press, London.
8   Shapiro, S.L., Carlson, L.E., Astin, J.A., and Freedman, B. (2006) Mechanisms of mindfulness. *Journal of Clinical Psychology*, 62 (3), 373–386.
9   Goleman, D. (1980) A map for inner space, in *Beyond Ego* (ed. R.N. Walsh and F. Vaughan), J.P. Tarcher, Los Angeles, pp. 141–150.

10 Kabat-Zinn, J. (2003) Mindfulness-based interventions in context: Past, present, and future. *Clinical Psychology: Science and Practice*, 10, 144–156.

11 Segal, Z.V., Williams, J.M.G., and Teasdale, J.D. (2002) *Mindfulness-Based Cognitive Therapy for Depression: A New Approach to Preventing Relapse*, Guilford Press, London.

2

What Is Mindfulness Practice?

What sort of practices might you learn in the context of a workplace mindfulness course and how might they be of benefit? The central practice on any mindfulness course is formal sitting meditation. Here, participants learn to still their minds and gain some calm – at least to some extent. But it's not easy to stop thinking about things and instead simply to pay attention to the changing flow of experience in the present moment. Try this simple experiment. Put this book to one side and, for just a minute or so, don't think of a white bear.

How did that go?

Not very well, I imagine. Most people trying that would think of white bears quite a bit. And what actually goes on for most people is more startling than you might imagine. In

The Mindful Workplace: Developing Resilient Individuals and Resonant Organizations with MBSR, First Edition. M. Chaskalson.
© 2011 John Wiley & Sons, Ltd. Published 2011 by John Wiley & Sons, Ltd.

an experiment published in 1987, the psychologist Daniel Wegner and colleagues[1] divided a group in two. One half was asked to try *not* to think of a white bear for five minutes and to ring a bell when they did. The other half was asked to think of a white bear *deliberately*. As you might expect, members of the group asked *not* to think of a white bear were unable to suppress the thought as they'd been instructed to. Then, *both* groups were asked to think about a white bear deliberately for another five minutes. The people who had been asked to suppress their thoughts of the bear at the outset showed significantly *more* thought about a white bear than did those who were asked to think about a white bear at the start. As shown by this and other studies,[2] what we resist persists. Our minds are hungry, always on the lookout for things to occupy themselves with and chew over from moment to moment to moment.

Maybe try another experiment now. Put this book aside again and, sitting still with your eyes closed, let your mind calm and let all your thoughts completely stop, just for a few minutes.

How did that one go? Again, probably not very well. Most of us quite naturally have a kind of monkey-mind. It hops around the leaves and branches of our awareness, thinking now about this, now about that, almost randomly. But if thought suppression doesn't work, how is it possible to calm our monkey-minds? How can we bring them to some kind of stillness, to a sustained, present-moment focus? A clue to the answer can be found in watching the behaviour of a young infant, completely absorbed in examining the palm of her hand, maybe for minutes on end. Human minds, it seems, have innate mechanisms that support sustained, vigilant and engaged attention. We just need to learn how to make use of these.

When we were much younger we did that quite naturally. Now, our minds have grown cluttered by the demands of daily life and our attention has become subsequently fragmented. Nowhere is this more true than at work, and the results of that fracturing of attention show up in the workplace in the form of wasteful mistakes, needless arguments, inefficiencies, duplicated effort, confusion and – perhaps above all – stress. The good news, though, is that you can train your mind by simply focusing and refocusing your wandering attention on a single object again and again and again, using the practice of meditation.

There are many different kinds of meditation and not all of them aim primarily to calm the mind and increase focus. With those that do have that aim, many different objects over the centuries have been used to focus the attention – a flickering candle flame, a coloured disk, a pebble, an inwardly and silently repeated sound or mantra, for example. In the context of MBSR courses, you begin by taking your breath as the object of attention. You just allow your attention to settle on the sensations that accompany each in-breath and each out-breath, just following the breath as it comes in and as it goes out. When the mind wanders, as it inevitably does, you notice where it went and then gently and kindly bring the attention back to the breath.

There are many advantages in using the breath as an object in this way. It's always there, for a start. You really can't leave home without it. It's also a kind of subtle barometer that allows you to measure the quality of your physical and emotional state. When you're tense or frightened you tend to hold your breath; when you're relaxed and at ease it flows more freely. Awareness of the breath can lead to a greater integration of the mind, body and emotions. Intentionally focusing on a single object can steady the mind.[3–5] When you do that, you activate the brain networks that correspond to the chosen object of attention and you inhibit the networks that correspond to competing demands for attention – without any need for force. It's as if the brain 'lights up' the selected object while also 'dimming' the unselected object.[6 (p. 76)] You can't force the mind to settle, but to take advantage of the mind's capacity to settle under certain circumstances, you do actually have to make an effort. You need to come back, again and again, to your original intention to have the mind settle on a chosen object. What is important here is the quality of the intention you engage. It has to be gentle.

Directing the spotlight of your attention onto the breath, you'll probably find that it settles there for a few moments before wandering away. So you refocus it, bringing it back to the breath again and again and again whenever you notice that it has wandered. The mind's tendency to wander in this way is not a mistake or a fault. It is the nature of the mind to wander – it's what minds do – and whenever you notice that yours has wandered you gently bring it back, over and over. This is very different from the attempt to forcibly fix the mind to a certain place – driving thoughts out or putting up barriers to unwanted feelings or body sensations. Instead, you employ a gentle, kind and gracious effort. The mind wanders, and you bring it back. It wanders, and you bring it back. If it wanders off a hundred times, you just bring it back a hundred times. Each time that you bring it back you're laying down deposits in the neural networks that are connected with sustained attention.[7]

All other things being equal, people who meditate grow bigger brains than those who don't. A study published by researchers at Harvard, Yale and MIT in 2005[8] revealed that experienced meditators showed increased thickness in parts of the brain that deal with attention and processing sensory input. These findings are consistent with what we have come to learn about the brain's inherent plasticity.[9] As you use your brain, so it changes. The mind has the capacity to sculpt and change different areas of the brain. London taxi drivers, who have to complete the enormous task of learning the location and layout of every street in the capital, grow a larger hippocampus – the part of the brain associated with the spatial memories that are needed for navigation.[10] Experienced violinists have structurally different cortical development in the areas associated with the manipulation of the fingers of the left hand (their usual fingering hand) from those who don't play the violin.[11]

This neuroplasticity – the changing of neurons in the brain, of the organization of their networks and of their function as we undertake new experiences – might be just what you would expect when you pause to think about it. If you want to build muscles you join a gym and lift weights again and again, building muscle by tiny increments with each movement. So it is with the brain. One of the key ideas in neuroplasticity is that neurons that fire together, wire together.[12] By using your mind in a particular way you grow and rewire the brain over time. Each time the mind wanders, each time you bring it back, you gradually build the neural networks involved in paying attention.

When you bring the attention back to the breath, again and again, the mind eventually begins to settle, at least for a little while. The traditional image for this is a flask of muddy water. Take a clear glass flask. Add some sand and some water and shake it up. As you hold it to the light all you see is brown murk. But leave it for a time and the sand begins to settle and the water grows clear and bright. Just sitting quietly in meditation for a while, with your eyes closed, your body still and without any deliberate attempt to think, speak or act, your mind eventually settles. But what may be even more important is that the *process* of doing this yields benefits that are as valuable as any calm result.

On an MBSR course, when the mind wanders you're invited to notice where it goes. If you're caught up in thinking, when you become aware of that you might just say to yourself: 'Ah, yes – there's thinking.' Or 'planning . . . ' or 'oh yes, anxious thoughts . . . ' and then you gently and kindly bring the attention back to the breath. There are several benefits in doing this. You begin to learn something about where your mind tends to go. You learn the pattern of your favourite preoccupations. You also develop an attitude of kindly forgiveness towards your recalcitrant mind. And you begin to develop metacognitive skills: every time you notice that you're thinking when your intention was to be following the breath, you have a moment of metacognitive awareness. The ability to know that you're thinking when you're thinking, that you're feeling when you're feeling, and that you're sensing when you're sensing is hugely valuable.

Although the shift in perspective is tiny, there is a world of difference between thinking irritated thoughts: 'No one here knows what they're doing! This team is completely useless! They're a waste of space!' And knowing that you're thinking irritated thoughts: 'Ah, right. Irritated thoughts . . . ' That metacognitive shift can be the cue that lets you calm down before doing anything rash. The metacognitive shift from being immersed in the experience, as a subject, to intimately observing the experience itself, as an object of your awareness, is one of the products of the MBSR approach. This capacity to know and accept your thoughts, feelings and body-sensations *as* thoughts, feelings and body-sensations is a potent agent for workplace well-being.[13] Raising your level of emotional intelligence,[14] it significantly enhances your cognitive capacities and your overall performance at work.[15]

Try this:

The Mindfulness of Breathing Meditation

Settling

Sit down on a comfortable straight-backed chair in a place where you won't be disturbed for a while. With your feet flat on the floor and your legs uncrossed, allow your back to rise up from the seat, maybe a little away from the back of the chair if that's comfortable, and let it fall naturally into an upright, alert and dignified posture.

Let your eyes close or, if you prefer to keep them open, let your gaze fall, unfocused, on the floor four or five feet away from you.

Bring your attention to your body. Maybe explore the sensations you find where your feet meet the floor – the sense of touch, pressure and contact there. Perhaps become aware of any sense of warmth or coolness at your feet.

Now let that awareness move up the body to the contact that's made between your body and the seat. Explore the pattern of sensations there. Feel your back, rising up from the seat. Let your chest open and your shoulders soften. With your chin tucked slightly down, the back of your neck lengthens.

Following the Breath

Become aware that you're breathing. Notice how each out-breath is followed by an in-breath; how each in-breath is followed by an out-breath. Your body knows just how to do this – how it wants to breathe right now, which is probably how it *is* breathing – so, letting the body breathe by itself, allow your attention gently to gather around the breath.

Just follow each in-breath, each out-breath. Notice the pauses between breaths. As best you can, keep your attention on the sensations that accompany the breath. Maybe a sense of slight tickling in the nostrils where the air passes over them. Maybe a sense of slight stretching in the belly as the air comes in, a sense of gentle release as it goes out. But, however and wherever you notice sensations, just keep your mind settled with the breath.

And When the Mind Wanders . . .

When the mind wanders it's not a mistake or a fault. It's just what minds do. So when you become aware that the mind has wandered, just notice where it went and then gently and kindly bring the attention back to the breath. If it helps you might inwardly say to yourself 'there's thinking . . . ' or 'there's planning . . . ' or whatever, and gently come back to the breath again.

Keep a gentle eye out for any tendency to self-critically judge how you're doing here. Notice the 'shoulds', the 'musts' and the 'oughts' that often turn up and, if they do, maybe just inwardly acknowledge them – 'Ah yes . . . judging . . . ' – and, gently and kindly, return your attention to the breath.

As best you can, bring a quality of kindness to your wandering mind. This is how we all are and it's OK. It's always possible to come back to the breath whenever the mind wanders and each time you do you take a tiny step forward in your practice.

Keep Following the Breath

Keep up this practice for 10 minutes or so (there's no need to time it precisely).

Ending

When you feel ready, open your eyes and come to move again, giving yourself a little time to come back to your normal mode of day-to-day consciousness.

The MBSR programme places a great deal of emphasis on the body, especially on the variety of sensations we experience in the body from moment to moment. There are many benefits to doing this. Awareness of what is happening in your body from moment to moment helps you to be more present with whatever is going on in the here and now. In the course of the day it's not uncommon to find your attention caught up in preoccupations with the past or in obsessions about the future – your plans and to-do list. If that happens you can bring your attention back to the present moment by becoming more consciously aware of the sensations where your feet meet the floor or of the feeling of breath moving in your abdomen.

Take the case of John, whose manager is trying to communicate important information to his team. Yet another PowerPoint . . . John's mind wanders: 'Will I pick up my dry-cleaning on the way home or leave it till tomorrow? And shall we book that holiday on the Internet tonight . . . Oh, I must arrange my time off . . . Who does this new guy remind me of? I mustn't forget to get that invoice off as soon as I get back to my desk . . . ' And so on. His body is in the meeting but his attention is miles away. John knows he's got a problem with concentration. People have told him that often enough and he struggles to stay present in meetings, but he can't seem to make himself do it. Just telling himself to concentrate, gritting his teeth and trying to force his mind to stay present and in one place, doesn't seem to work.

With a bit of training, John could learn to bring his attention more readily into the present moment by becoming aware of one or another physical sensation, by following his breath for a few moments, or by finding something that interests him in the present moment. For where there is interest, the attention naturally settles, without any need for force or control. A key here is learning to take an interest, how to be curious about events in the body and the mind in the present moment. The cultivation of that attitude of curiosity is a key component in mindfulness training.

Awareness of what is happening in your body from moment to moment also helps you to monitor changes in your state of mind. Participants on mindfulness courses sometimes discover that they have long-standing physical habits of which they've been largely unconscious – clenching their fists or locking their jaws when they're tense, for example – and these can go largely unnoticed. When you become more aware of your body through mindfulness training you can take more conscious steps to change things. Noticing that you're feeling tense, for example, you can take a two-minute walk to ease the tension, or pause for a drink, or just follow the breath for a minute.

Finally, we all know what it is like to get caught up in dysfunctional or unhelpful patterns of thought. Take the example of Raj, who is ploughing through his email inbox, making great progress in dealing with the backlog, when he's hit by a sudden thought. 'That email I sent before lunch . . . Did I attach the right file?' Checking back through his 'sent' folder, he finds the email. No attachment. 'Oh no! That was so stupid! How could I do that? I *keep* making blunders like that. What are they going to think of me? My credibility is going to be completely blown by this. They'll never take me seriously. I spent so long getting the draft just right. Now they'll think I'm just a joker . . . ' On and on and on he goes – beating himself up, bringing his mood down, cycling around the situation over and over, losing more and more creativity with every iteration of the story.

With some mindfulness training Raj might have approached that differently. Finding himself caught up in a compulsive loop of self-critical catastrophizing, he could have moved his attention very deliberately to the churning sensations in his belly. Breathing into these, breathing with them, just exploring these sensations for one or two minutes, he could have shifted some of his mind's 'central-processor resources' away from thoughts and into the body. Breaking open the cycle of self-recrimination in this way, he might have found that, in a very short space of time, his catastrophizing thoughts began to subside. That would have allowed him to take a more creative perspective on the situation and make a more resourceful choice about what to do next. By moving your attention away from your thoughts and engaging it with body sensations, you can often move quite readily from distressing and dysfunctional patterns of thought.[16]

One of the practices taught early on in the MBSR programme is the body-scan meditation. In this practice you move your attention, consciously and deliberately, around the body, exploring the detailed nature of present-moment sensation in each part. The body scan helps you to become more familiar with the variety of sensations in your body as they actually are from moment to moment. Much of the time we go about with an *idea* of our bodies that isn't linked to the actual *experience* of our bodies. By practising the body scan you come to be much more aware of the changing sensations in your body from moment to moment. You also develop a greater capacity to deliberately move your attention to where you want it to be and to keep it there for a while.

Try this:

The Body-Scan Meditation

Lie down, making yourself comfortable, on a mat or a rug on the floor or on your bed, in a place where you will be warm and undisturbed, and allow your eyes gently to close.

Feel the movement of your breath and become aware of the sensations in your body. Take your time to settle and, when you're ready, begin to explore your changing physical sensations, right now. Start with the sense of touch and pressure where your body contacts whatever you're lying on. With each out-breath, let yourself sink deeper into that.

The intention of this practice is to be awake and aware, not to fall asleep. It isn't intended to help you feel different – more relaxed, or calm. That may happen, or it may not. Rather, the aim of the practice is to become more aware, feeling all the different sensations you detect, in this moment, as you focus your attention on different parts of the body in turn.

Many of us today suffer from low-level sleep deprivation and, if you do the body scan lying down, it's very easy to fall asleep. That might be refreshing, and if you *do* fall asleep for a few moments you can always just pick the practice up again. But you might also find it helps to prop your head up with a pillow, open your eyes, or do the practice sitting up rather than lying down.

When you're settled, start by becoming aware of the sensations in your belly, feeling the changing patterns of sensation there as you breathe in and out. Take a few minutes really to feel and explore those sensations.

Then bring the focus of your awareness to the toes of your left foot. Focus on each of the toes in turn, bringing a warm, kindly curiosity to the sensations you find there. Not *thinking about* the toes – just noticing the actual experience of whatever sensations you find there. Maybe you notice the sensation of contact between the toes, or feel a sense of tingling or warmth or numbness: whatever's there. And if there's no sensation there that's fine too – whatever you experience is OK, it's just what's here, right now – and that's the point.

Then, on an in-breath, feel or imagine the breath entering the lungs and passing down the body, down the left leg, to the toes of the left foot. And, on the out-breath, feel or imagine the breath coming back up from the toes, up the leg, up the torso and out through the nose. Imaginatively and experimentally, as best you can, breathe in this way for a few breaths: down to the toes on each in-breath, back up from the toes on each out-breath.

Then, when you are ready, on an out-breath, let go of awareness of the toes and bring your awareness to the sensations on the sole of your left foot. With a kind and gentle curiosity, investigate what you discover on the sole of the foot. Then the instep and heel – noticing, perhaps, the sensations of touch and contact where the heel meets the floor or whatever you're lying on. Experiment with 'breathing with' these sensations – aware of the breath in the background as you explore sensations in the foreground.

Then, let your awareness expand to the rest of the foot – the ankle, the top of the foot, the outside of the foot – and allow the focus of awareness to move on to the lower left leg – the calf, the shin, the knee and so on in turn.

Keep scanning the body in this way, staying for a time with each part of it. Left shin, left knee, left thigh . . . right toes, right foot and ankle, lower right leg, right knee, right thigh . . . the pelvic region, buttocks and hips . . . lower back and belly, upper back and chest. Then move on to the hands, both at the same time. Explore the sensations in the fingers and thumbs, then the palms, the backs of the hands, the wrists, lower arms and elbows, upper arms . . . the shoulders, the neck and the face (jaw, mouth, lips, nose, cheeks, ears, eyes, forehead), and, finally, the head as a whole.

When you become aware of tension, or any other intense sensation in any part of the body, you can 'breathe in' to that sensation – gently using the in-breath to bring awareness right into the sensation and releasing and letting go on the out-breath.

From time to time the mind will wander. That's only natural. When you notice that it's wandered, just acknowledge it, noting where it went, and then – gently and kindly – bring your attention to whatever part of the body you were last aware of.

When you've scanned the whole body in this way, spend a few minutes feeling the body as a whole, aware of the breath flowing in and out before getting up and carrying on with your day. As best you can, bring whatever mindfulness you've cultivated in this practice to whatever comes next.

Mindful Movement

Meditations like the mindfulness of breathing and the body scan take place in a kind of controlled environment. You find a space that is warm and quiet, where you won't be disturbed and where you can close your eyes and engage in the practice for a significant amount of time – 10 to 50 minutes, perhaps. But mindfulness is not the same as meditation and, wonderful though these controlled 'laboratory conditions' for meditation are, as you begin to work more deliberately with your mind and your physical and mental states, mindfulness also needs to be practised 'live', in the moment-by-moment flow of daily life.

The mindful-movement practices that form part of the MBSR course are usually drawn from disciplines such as yoga or qigong. Apart from the obvious physical benefits these bring by way of stretching and strengthening previously underused muscles and joints, they are also a way of bringing more mindfulness into the body and its movements. They are therefore nearer to the experience of mindfulness in daily life. But, more than that, they are also an opportunity to 'work the edge'. By that we mean that these practices give you the opportunity to see what happens when your body and mind come upon a point of automatic, and often unconscious, resistance. Coming to the edge of your usual comfort zone, you can tend to pull back and try to return to comfort. But in these practices you try not to do that. Instead, you're encouraged to explore the edge, to see what's there and what it's like, gently and kindly bringing curiosity to the experience. Opening to it, you learn to allow what's there simply to be what's there.

Try this:

Mindful-Movement Practice

With all the mindful-movement practices it's very important to take care of yourself and always allow the wisdom of your own body to override any instruction that may be given. Especially if there are any health or other difficulties that might make standing for long periods or stretching and bending unwise, it's important to make an informed choice about whether and how to do these.

That said, there can also be a natural human tendency to pull back from discomfort, and part of the value of these practices is to find another way of being with what's difficult, without always pulling back.

If it's right for you, come to stand with feet shoulder-width apart, parallel and pointing forwards. Keeping the knees unlocked, tilt the pelvis slightly forward – tucking the tailbone in. Let the belly soften, the chest open and the shoulders ease, allowing the arms simply to hang by your sides. With the chin tucked slightly down, the back of the neck lengthens.

Stand for a few moments, feeling the feet making a strong contact with the floor: grounded, present, alert. Let the breath come and go as it does, just letting the body breathe itself.

After a few moments, bring your arms out from your sides, pointing your hands and fingers away from the body towards the opposite sides of the room. Your arms should be stretching out at shoulder level and parallel to the floor.

There should now be a more or less straight line from the tips of the fingers, across the arms and shoulders and through the base of the neck.

Really reach out with your fingers, pressing outwards away from the body.

Check that you're still breathing easily. Look for any tensing, any bracing, any frowning and release these if you find them.

Now, as best you can, holding the arms where they are, lift the fingers upwards towards the ceiling. Stretching the fingers upwards, press outwards with the palms and feel that stretch right across the back of the arms and into the hands and fingers.

Notice any tendency here to want to pull back and release the stretch. Maybe explore this edge. Is it possible simply to stay with any experience of discomfort, any burning or stretching sensation, perhaps, for just a few moments more? As best you can, bring a kind of affectionate enquiry and curiosity to what you find. What exactly are these sensations like? Where are they more intense, where less intense?

Then, when it seems right, release the stretch and let the arms float down to your sides again. Stand for a few moments and feel what has changed. What is this moment like, now?

The capacity to work the edge in this way is an important part of the training on an MBSR course. By learning to bring a kindly curiosity to the experience of difficulties in the body, participants may find that they can begin to bring the same attitude to other difficult experiences, learning how to be with difficulty without always reacting to it. It's easy to see how an increased capacity to be with what is difficult in this way, allowing it, letting it be, can have significant benefits in the workplace. Imagine the case of Louise, who tends to react with inner and unexpressed hostility every time anyone gives her what she thinks of as a command. She doesn't know why she does that, but she feels it. When that happens, she grits her teeth, bites back a cutting response and gets on with her job. But it saps her energy. On the surface things seem to be going OK but the result is that she often performs under par.

It's not that she works in an especially hierarchical setting. She just has these reactions. She's touchy in this area. Maybe it goes back to her childhood.

After doing an MBSR course Louise might notice that tendency. She might become aware of how she clenches her teeth at such times, how her stomach tightens whenever she feels she's been given an order. Instead of reacting in that way, she might learn simply to register the discomfort and sit with it for a few moments. In that space, she might ask herself: 'Was this person unreasonable, seeming to tell me what to do?' She might, of course, conclude that it was unreasonable, in which case a useful discussion might follow. But she might sometimes see that she was just reacting, just having her buttons pressed, and she might be able to let that go and move on more creatively.

Or take the case of Phil. He sticks rigidly to his job description – just that and no more. When people are off sick or there's another emergency on, Phil hangs back. He works within safe, known boundaries. Any attempt to get him to step outside of these meets with resistance. He simply hates the discomfort of stepping into the unknown. He doesn't do it. Or if he does, it's with enormous inner trepidation and reluctance. With some mindfulness training Phil might come to see his resistance for what it is – a fear of the unknown. He might learn to explore the feelings, thoughts and body sensations that occur when he meets an edge – at least to some extent. That might allow him to be a bit more courageous in his approach, to extend himself that bit further. As a result he might become more productive at work. He might also experience higher levels of job satisfaction. The capacity to work the edge and to be with discomfort in that way can make for remarkable changes in attitude and outlook.

Mindful Walking

There are four traditional meditation postures: sitting, as in the mindfulness of breathing meditation; lying, as in the body scan; standing, as in the mindful movement; and now we come to the final posture – walking.

Walking meditations have often accompanied sitting practice. On longer meditation retreats, for instance, people alternate sitting with walking meditation over many hours of practice. Forty minutes of sitting, ten or twenty minutes of walking, over and over. In that case you would approach the practice fairly formally, as described below.

With a little bit of practice of mindful walking in the formal way described above, it might soon become easier to drop into an awareness of the sensations of walking during daily life.

Try this:

Mindful-Walking Practice

Find a place where you can walk up and down for perhaps 10 to 20 paces. It can be inside or outside, but in this formal practice it's important that you won't be disturbed by other people or concerned that you might be seen if you don't want to be.

Stand with your feet parallel, a little apart, and your knees unlocked. Let your arms hang at your sides and direct your gaze to the ground, five or six feet ahead of you, letting the focus soften.

Stand for a few moments, breathing.

Become aware of the sensations at your feet, especially where the soles of your feet meet the ground, and feel the weight of your body moving down through the legs and feet, and down through any building you may be in, down to the earth.

Maybe flex the knees a few times and flex the feet to get a clearer sense of the sensations in the feet and legs.

When you're ready, let the left heel slowly lift, feeling any sensations in the foot and calf muscles as you do that, and continue to lift, letting the whole of the left foot come off the ground, as the weight moves completely to the right leg. Stay aware of the sensations in the left foot and leg as you gently move it forward, letting the left heel contact the ground. Let the rest of the left foot now make contact with the ground and feel the weight of the body moving forward onto the left leg and foot, as the right heel comes up off the ground.

With the weight now on the left leg, let the right foot lift and move slowly forward, staying aware of the changing patterns of sensations in the foot and leg as you do that. Keep your attention on the right heel as it contacts the ground. Feel the weight shifting forward onto the right foot as it meets the ground and feel the left heel rising up again.

Slowly move in this way for between 10 and 20 paces, keeping especially aware of the sensations in the soles of the feet and heels as they make contact with the ground, and feeling the sensations in the muscles of the legs as they move.

When it's time to make a turn, come slowly around, appreciating the complex pattern of movements through which the body changes direction, and now walk in the opposite direction.

Walk up and down in this way for a while. Stay aware, as best you can, of the sensations in the feet and legs, focusing especially on the contact of the feet with the ground.

When you become aware that the mind has wandered away from the sensations of walking, gently move it back to the sensations in the feet and legs, using the sensations where the feet meet the ground as an 'anchor', a way of coming back to the present moment, just as you used the breath in the sitting meditation.

If the mind is very agitated, it may be helpful to stop for a moment, and just stand, breathing, until both mind and body re-stabilize themselves and you resume the mindful walking.

Keep walking for 10 to 15 minutes, or longer if you wish.

At first, walk at a pace that is slower than usual to give yourself a better chance to be fully aware of the sensations of walking. When you feel more comfortable walking slowly and with awareness, you can experiment with walking faster – up to and beyond normal walking speed. If you're feeling agitated, it might be helpful to begin walking fast, with awareness, and then slow down as you begin to settle.

That opens up opportunities for mindful practice in the working day. When you get up from your desk to visit a colleague on another floor, for example, or to fetch a drink, you can practise some mindful walking. The walk from your car to your desk, or a walk on the way to the office – to the station or the bus stop perhaps – all these can be good opportunities to practise mindful walking. Such simple practices, fitting naturally into the flow of the working day, can have a significant impact on your vitality at work. Just refreshing yourself from time to time – coming away from the endless flow of thoughts and attending to the sensations of the body moving for a few moments – can be enormously invigorating.

Mindfulness of Routine Activities

As we've seen, it's possible to be mindful while sitting, standing, walking and lying down, and there are formal meditation practices associated with each of these postures. But mindfulness can extend beyond such formal practices into every aspect of daily life. To get a sense of that, participants on MBSR courses are encouraged, as part of their homework on the course, deliberately to practise mindfulness of a few everyday activities.

One such practice is to have the experience, just once, of eating a single meal mindfully, with the same quality of attention that was brought to the raisin exercise. It's best here to choose a simple meal – a bowl of muesli, perhaps, or a sandwich or a piece of fruit. Really pay attention to each aspect of the meal, letting all your senses fully engage with the process and noticing what you discover in each moment as you proceed.

Another practice is the mindfulness of routine activities. Here, you choose a routine activity – something you do every day – and you make a deliberate effort to bring moment-to-moment awareness to that activity each time you do it. Again, you try and bring the same quality of mindful attention to that activity as you did with the raisin exercise. Possibilities include your first cup of tea or coffee, brushing your teeth, showering, drying yourself, getting dressed, your walk to the bus, train or car, eating – anything that you do every day. The aim here is to pay detailed attention to each element in the experience, making a point of knowing what you are doing as you're actually doing it.

It's not easy to do these simple practices. In the early stages of an MBSR course, participants often report that they simply forget to do them. And when they do remember, they often find that their minds wander off halfway through a simple two-minute activity and they forget to bring the mind back. This last point highlights the place of working memory in the practice of mindfulness. A sustained, more or less coherent working memory is crucial for the fulfilment of many work-related tasks. But the incessant demands of working life today, with the relentless flow of emails, calls, meetings and other demands, fractures and scrambles working memory. Quite simply, we forget to pay attention. Mindfulness training increases your capacity to maintain a degree of sustained working memory.[7] It increases your capacity to keep your attention on the task in hand. With training, you can simply be more mindful as you go about your day. That means you can attend to your tasks in a more sustained way. But, more than that, it also means that you're more able to be awake and aware of yourself, others and the world around you. It lets you be right here, right now, getting the most from this fleeting day, this fleeting life.

References

1   Wegner, D.M., Schneider, D.J., Carter, S.R., and White, T.L. (1987) Paradoxical effects of thought suppression. *Journal of Personality and Social Psychology*, 53 (1), 5–13.

2   Wenzlaff, R.M., and Wegner, D.M. (2000) Thought suppression. *Annual Review of Psychology*, 51, 59–91.

3   Laberge, D. (2008) Computational and anatomical models of selective attention in object identification, in *Cognitive Neuroscience: The Biology of the Mind* (ed. M.S. Gazzaniga), W.W. Norton & Company, New York, pp. 649–663.

4   Duncan, J. (2004) Selective attention in distributed brain systems, in *Cognitive Neuroscience of Attention* (ed. M.I. Posner), Guilford Press, New York, pp. 105–113.

5   Posner, M.I., and Rothbart, M.K. (1991) Attentional mechanisms and conscious experience, in *The Neuropsychology of Consciousness* (ed. A.D. Milner and M.D. Rugg), Academic Press, London, pp. 91–112.

6   Williams, M., Teasdale, J., Segal, S., and Kabat-Zinn, J. (2007) *The Mindful Way through Depression: Freeing Yourself from Chronic Unhappiness*, Guilford Press, London.

7   Jha, A.P., Krompinger, J., and Baime, M.J. (2007) Mindfulness training modifies subsystems of attention. *Cognitive, Affective, & Behavioral Neuroscience*, 7 (2), 109–119.

8   Lazar, S.W., Kerr, C.E., Wasserman, R.H., *et al.* (2005) Meditation experience is associated with increased cortical thickness. *Neuroreport*, 16 (17), 1893–1897.

9   Konorski, J. (1948) *Conditioned Reflexes and Neuron Organization*, Cambridge University Press, Cambridge.

10 Maguire, E.A., Gadian, D.G., Johnsrude, I.S., *et al.* (2000) Navigation-related structural change in the hippocampi of taxi drivers. *Proceedings of the National Academy of Sciences*, 97 (8), 4398–4403.

11 Elbert, T., Pantev, C., Wienbruch, C., *et al.* (1995) Increased cortical representation of the fingers of the left hand in string players. *Science*, 270, 305–307.

12 Hebb, D.O. (1949) *The Organization of Behavior: A Neuropsychological Theory*, Wiley & Sons, Inc., New York.

13 Donaldson-Feilder, E.J., and Bond, F.W. (2004) The relative importance of psychological acceptance and emotional

intelligence to workplace well-being. *British Journal of Guidance and Counselling*, 32 (2), 187–203.

14 Briñol, P., Petty, R.E., and Rucker, D.D. (2006) The role of meta-cognitive processes in emotional intelligence. *Psicothema*, 18 (S), 26–33.

15 Lam, L.T., and Kirby, S.L. (2002) Is emotional intelligence an advantage? An exploration of the impact of emotional and general intelligence on individual performance. *Journal of Social Psychology*, 142 (1), 133–143.

16 Segal, Z.V., Williams, J.M.G., and Teasdale, J.D. (2002) *Mindfulness-Based Cognitive Therapy for Depression: A New Approach to Preventing Relapse*, Guilford Press, London.

3

Positive and Negative Stress
Up and Down the
Yerkes–Dodson Curve

Working life is often stressful and it can be hard in some
workplace cultures to acknowledge that. Over the past few
years I've been contacted by phone on several occasions by
workplace managers and others who have enquired about the
public stress-reduction courses I run and the conversation has
gone something like this:

CLIENT:	I've read an article in a magazine about the stress-reduction work you do. Can you tell me something about that?
MICHAEL:	Certainly. But before I begin, can you tell me a little about yourself? What brings you to the course?
CLIENT:	Well, I'm group head of taxation at XYZ multinational and it's been really stressful there lately.

*The Mindful Workplace: Developing Resilient Individuals and Resonant Organizations
with MBSR*, First Edition. M. Chaskalson.
© 2011 John Wiley & Sons, Ltd. Published 2011 by John Wiley & Sons, Ltd.

I'm looking for something that might help me with that.

MICHAEL: OK – that's fine. The course I run might well help with that. But before we go ahead and do the booking, can I just check – is there anything your firm puts on that might help you with this?

CLIENT: Well, no – not really. I guess I could contact occupational health and discuss it with them, but that seems to be more for acute cases and that doesn't fit my experience. I'd just like something that would help me to manage the stress better – to be more effective. We've got nothing like that here.

Some corporate cultures in the United Kingdom today seem to expect their people to be superhuman, able to deal easily with whatever their world throws at them. In this they're living a painful delusion that results in the loss to the economy of hundreds of millions of pounds each year.[i] Part of the problem is a failure to distinguish between pressure and stress.

The Yerkes–Dodson Curve

The diagram in Figure 3.1, variants of which are often found to accompany a discussion of the relation between stress and output, is usually attributed to the psychologists Robert Yerkes and John Dodson.[1] An article they published in 1908[2] is taken as a standard description of the relationship between stress and performance. As pressure on us increases, so our capacity to respond to that pressure – to perform – increases, but only up to a point. Beyond a certain point, if the pressure continues unabated, our performance starts to fall off. And if that con-

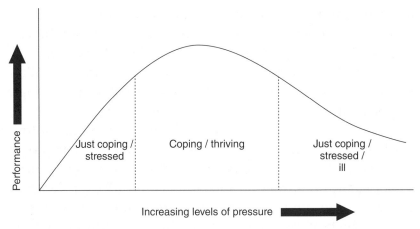

Figure 3.1 The Yerkes–Dodson Curve.

tinues for much longer, we become stressed and eventually we begin to get ill. Thyroid or endocrine burnout, obesity, diabetes, the inability to experience pleasure from normally pleasurable events, immune suppression, psoriasis, lupus, fibromyalgia, chronic fatigue, chronic pain, cancer, heart disease, infertility and irritable bowel syndrome or other digestive disorders – all of these may be connected to the ongoing experience of stress.[3] Stress can kill. No one is exempt from this. You can't buck the Yerkes–Dodson Law.

There is a relationship between the Yerkes–Dodson Law, as it's commonly interpreted, and the idea of flow, as described by the positive psychologist Mihály Csíkszentmihályi.[4] For Csíkszentmihályi, flow represents the way people speak of their state of mind when their consciousness is harmoniously ordered and they want to pursue whatever they are doing for its own sake. One of the preconditions for flow is the appropriate balance between personal resources and challenge. If the task you are engaged in calls for more personal resources than are available to you, you become stressed. If it makes

59

fewer demands on you than you are capable of, you become bored (and persistent boredom can itself be stressful). You need to find and maintain a point of optimum balance.

Coming back to the Yerkes–Dodson Curve and its relation to stress in the workplace – if people aren't given enough responsibility, if their work makes too few demands on them, that will be stressful as they struggle to get by at the bottom left-hand part of the curve. As more is asked of them and as they respond to the challenge, they begin to ascend the curve – coping OK or, further on, enjoying the positive challenge of the work. The pressure here is positively stimulating, bringing out the best in people, getting them to perform well. At this point you are dancing around the peak, perhaps even enjoying periods of flow. But if the pressure continues to build, without let up, you can all too easily tip beyond that point and enter the domain of stress.

This kind of thing happens at all levels of organizational life. In *Seeing Systems*,[5] Barry Oshry describes the core systemic dynamics that lead to personal and organizational dysfunction. There are four broadly defined positions (or conditions) that you can occupy at different times and in different contexts in your relationship to an organization. At different times and in different circumstances you may be:

Top – having overall responsibility for a significant part of your work or organization;

Middle – caught between conflicting demands and priorities from above and below;

Bottom – mainly subject to initiatives over which you have no control;

Customer – in need of some other group or person for a product or service that you require.

In our relationship to organizations we constantly move in and out of Top, Middle, Bottom and Customer conditions. The patterns of our relationships then unfold something like this:

> Tops are burdened by what feels like unmanageable complexity;
> Bottoms are oppressed by what they see as distant and uncaring Tops;
> Middles are torn and confused between the conflicting demands and priorities coming at them from Tops and Bottoms;
> Customers feel done-to by nonresponsive delivery systems.
>
> Top teams are caught up in destructive turf warfare;
> Middle peers are alienated from one another, non-cooperative and competitive;
> Bottom group members are trapped in stifling pressures to conform.
>
> Tops are fighting fires when they should be shaping the system's future;
> Middles are isolated from one another when they should be working together to coordinate system processes;
> Bottoms' negative feelings toward Tops and Middles distract them from putting their creative energies into the delivery of products and services;
> Customers' disgruntlement with the system keeps them from being active partners in helping the system produce the products and services they need.
>
> Throughout the system there is personal stress, relationship breakdowns, and severe limitations in the system's capacity to do what it intends to.[5] (pp. xiii–xiv)

For Oshry, the key way out of these various impasses is the development of insight into the endemic nature of complex systems. Whatever one makes of that, from the mindfulness perspective there is no doubt that a greater capacity to be *aware* of what you experience inside yourself – your body, mind, heart and spirit – and to pay full attention to what is happening around you – with other people, your surroundings and events – will significantly enhance your capacity to navigate the stressful complexities of organizational life.

In 1975 the endocrinologist Hans Selye[6] coined the word 'eustress' (the Greek *eu* means 'well' or 'good' – thus 'good stress') when he published a model dividing stress into two categories: eustress and distress. Persistent stress that is not resolved through coping or adaptation leads to 'distress', which gives rise in time to anxiety or depression. But stress can also enhance physical or mental function, for instance through strength training or challenging work. In that case it is eustress.

In an interview published in the *Harvard Business Review*, Herbert Benson[7] – a researcher in the field of neuroscience and stress – discussed the difference between distress and eustress. Stress itself is the physiological response to any change – good or bad – that alerts the adaptive fight-or-flight response in the brain and body. Elite athletes, creative artists and all high achievers will often experience this as eustress, as will anyone who has clinched an important deal or had a good performance review. All of these are accompanied by clear thinking, focus and creative insight. But when most people talk about stress they mean distress. At work, this refers to the negative stressors that arise from the actions of customers, clients, bosses, colleagues and employees – as well as demanding deadlines. Along with these stressors, at the medical institute that he runs, Benson also encounters executives who worry incessantly about the changing world economy, the impact of uncontrollable events on their markets and sources of finance, the world oil supply, family problems, taxes, traffic jams, hurricanes, child abductions, terrorist attacks and environmental devastation.

Organizational life can be tough and it is a huge human tragedy that, under such circumstances, the issue of stress has become so taboo that many people never learn how best to manage it. For Benson, the key to managing stress, to managing the Yerkes–Dodson Curve when you're at its peak, is learning to elicit what he calls a 'relaxation response' – a physical state of deep rest that counteracts the harmful effects of the fight-or-flight response that we're all familiar with. When you encounter a stressor at work – a difficult boss, employee or colleague, a tough negotiation, a tight deadline – you can deal with it for a while and then negative effects set in. In time, your sympathetic nervous system can become overloaded. The mechanisms that come into play here are part of our evolutionary heritage. We are here, quite literally, because we're on a hair trigger to register threat in our environment and to respond quickly and appropriately to that. If our ancestors roaming the plains and forest where wild bears and other predators abounded hadn't been so well adapted to react to threat, we'd not be here today.

When you meet a threat or any other stressor, a set of hormones is released into the bloodstream and the sympathetic nervous system is activated (see Figure 3.2). If you were out in the woods hunting 20 000 years ago, this would have served you really well. If you had caught sight of the tail of a bear behind a nearby rock, one of these sets of hormones – adrenalin and noradrenalin – would have immediately raised your blood pressure, directing blood flow primarily to the large

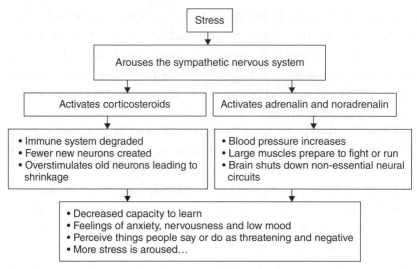

Figure 3.2 The sympathetic nervous system.

muscle groups, preparing your body for fighting or running away. Other hormones, the corticosteroids, would have been released to help deal with any physical damage that might have come from the encounter, such as wounds or inflamed and swollen muscles. At the same time, your brain would have shut down non-essential neural circuits – you don't need to be thinking about the meaning of existence when you're being chased by a bear!

Stress responses are a crucial part of our survival mechanism. If we didn't have them we'd be run over by buses. The trouble is, these days, when we aren't threatened by bears and threats are far less serious, the sympathetic nervous system can be stimulated by thoughts like, 'Did I attach the document to the email I just sent?', or 'I'm going to have to present my thinking to a group of 30 senior people and I don't feel quite ready . . . ' Even imagined events can stimulate the sympathetic nervous system, and once stimulated it produces a variety of physiological responses. And so, ironically, the mere thought of presenting your work to a group of senior people can pump your limbs with blood so that you're ready to run or fight and flood your system with the chemicals you'll need to recover from bites and bruises – but organizational life isn't quite like that these days.

As we've seen, under some circumstances the physiological effects of stressors are benign. You get going. Under some circumstances you may experience eustress. But, depending on the extent of sympathetic-nervous-system activation, you may also experience a racing heart, digestive difficulties, muscle tension, headaches, hyperventilation, excessive perspiration, agitation, anxiety, disturbed sleep and changed appetite. If the sympathetic nervous system is chronically activated, stress becomes distress and you may begin to experience trouble concentrating, to have difficulty in making decisions and have problems with remembering, as well as to suffer from fatigue, lack of energy or motivation and frequent illness.

The long-term physiological effects of sympathetic overload are dangerous. If stimulated for too long, the sympathetic nervous system degrades the immune system. It inhibits the production of new neurons in the brain and stimulates older neurons, causing shrinkage and even the death of brain tissue. In this state, you become less able to learn and take in new experiences. An over-stimulated amygdala, the part of the brain that detects threat in your environment, leaves you feeling anxious, nervous, stressed and even depressed. You may feel you are losing control and that the things people do or say are threatening and negative. Your body and mind lose resilience and creativity and you begin to see the world as threatening. You may begin to stop doing the things that actively help you to regain your equilibrium and you can enter what the psychologist Professor Marie Asberg has called an exhaustion funnel.[8] [(p. 28)]

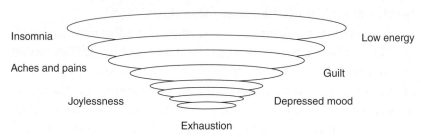

Figure 3.3   The exhaustion funnel.

The narrowing of the circles in Figure 3.3 illustrates the narrowing of life as we give up the things that we enjoy but which seem to be optional. We stop doing the things that nourish us, leaving only work and other stressors that continue to deplete our resources. It needn't get to this – and if it already has, there is a way out.

If the sympathetic nervous system is the body's accelerator, the parasympathetic nervous system is its brake. They work in complement to one another and one of the main functions of the parasympathetic nervous system is to mediate the effects of the sympathetic nervous system. In more primitive times, stressful events like hunting or fighting were usually followed by longer periods of rest – gathering food or doing uneventful routine work. One would tan hides, make tools, eat, play and socialize with friends and family. During such times the parasympathetic nervous system is activated and one begins to renew oneself and recover from stress. Renewal[9] begins when benign experiences arouse the parasympathetic nervous system. Another set of hormones is now released into the bloodstream, including oxytocin, which enhances social bonding, and vasopressin, which lowers blood pressure. There is an increased secretion of immunoglobulin A and natural killer-cell production is enhanced, strengthening the immune system. The hippocampus is stimulated, improving memory and allowing for new learning. One begins to feel elated, happy, optimistic, positive or amused. In this state, you are likely to experience events as generally positive rather than threatening or negative (Figure 3.4).

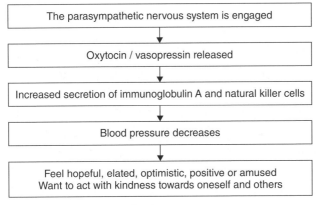

Figure 3.4 The parasympathetic nervous system.

Benson asserts that at the peak of the Yerkes–Dodson Curve, if one deliberately evokes a parasympathetic response by turning to a rejuvenating activity, a benign and creative set of physiological responses takes place.[7] These include the production of neurotransmitters such as endorphins and dopamine that enhance your general feeling of well-being. As the brain quietens down under these circumstances, Benson and his team have noticed an increased activity in the areas of brain associated with attention, space–time concepts and decision-making. As a result, you may experience a sudden creative insight in which the solution to a problem becomes obvious. After that, Benson says, you enter a 'new-normal' state because that breakthrough becomes part of your new mental mechanism. At the peak of the Yerkes–Dodson Curve, if you are consciously able to move for a short time into a receptive, relaxed state, you may discover a state of much higher neurological performance than would otherwise be the case. People who do this as a matter of course perform at consistently higher levels. The effect, says Benson, is particularly noticeable in athletes and creative artists. But he and his team have also seen it in the business people they work with.

The intriguing question, then, is: how do you do this? How do you deliberately elicit a parasympathetic response and move from a state of high alertness into a state of relaxation? How do you develop and sustain eustress and prevent it from moving into distress? Mindfulness training can certainly help. Mindfulness is much more than a simple relaxation response – it involves a heightened sense of present-moment awareness: awareness of yourself, of others and of the world around you. It is also a way of being much more 'present' to your own experience – right here, right now, from moment to moment. A greater capacity to do this – to be more aware of your thoughts, feelings and body sensations from moment to moment, to be more aware of the world around you and to be able to direct your attention more at will – would certainly leave you better able to manage your journey up and down the Yerkes–Dodson Curve.

Try this:

The Mindful Minute

None of us is so busy that we can't spare a minute from time to time. Literally, one minute. Just one. When you're waiting for the train in the morning, or waiting for the bus; when you arrive at your desk or you're waiting for your computer to boot . . . Just one single minute.

There's a really effective meditation practice you can do that lasts exactly one minute. It's extraordinarily handy and portable and you can fit it in pretty much anywhere – even the lavatory at work if you can't find anywhere else.

When you do this practice for the first time you'll need to time yourself for exactly one minute. You can use an egg timer for this, or ask a friend to time you, or go to http://timberfrog.com/countdown/, where you will find a handy online countdown timer.

The meditation here is very similar to the mindfulness of breathing which has already been described, but this time, instead of just watching each breath, you set out to count them. You let the breath just breathe itself, in whatever way you normally breathe, and you pay particular attention to each breath – counting at the end of each out-breath. You just count each breath you take over the course of exactly one timed minute so that – at the end – you'll know precisely how many breaths you take in a minute.

Begin by sitting in a chair with your feet square on the floor in front of you and your body arranged more or less symmetrically. Find a posture that is relaxed, upright and dignified. Then, closing your eyes, bring your attention to the breath and begin to follow each in-breath and each out-breath. Do that for a few breaths and, when you feel you have a sense of the breath moving in the body, start your one-minute timer and begin to count your breaths.

Breathe in, breathe out, and (mentally) count 'one'. Breathe in, breathe out, and count 'two'. Breathe in, breathe out, and count 'three' . . . and so on. Keep going for exactly one minute. Then, when your timer sounds or your friend calls time, remember what number you were on.

People vary, and the number of breaths you take in one minute is neither here nor there for our purposes. The main thing is to remember how many breaths you took in that minute: 6, 10, 14, 18 or whatever. That way, when you've got a minute to spare and you want to become more mindful you can set out to count your 6 or 18 breaths – whatever you found.

You can do this before an important phone call or before getting out of the car on your way to an important meeting. You can do it as a preparation for a presentation or as a way of getting yourself back to centre after a disturbing encounter. You can do it pretty much anywhere, any time and for whatever reason. If you dot a few of these through your day it will make things run better – whatever you're doing.

I was once working with a chief executive at a financial-services company. His part of the larger global company wasn't getting the results that the parent company was looking for and my client was asked to move on. A member of the parent company's board flew into London to have a meeting with him to discuss his severance package. My client later told me that, during the four-hour negotiation that ensued, he excused himself and went to the lavatory four times. There, each time, he did a one-minute meditation before returning to the negotiation.

He attributes the enormously generous settlement package he was finally given to those mindful minutes. The mindful minute is a really effective practice. It can help you better regulate your journey up and down the Yerkes–Dodson Curve, making you calmer and more centred, more effective and easier to be with. It can even, as in the case of my client, make you rich.

Note

i For 2005/2006 the UK Health and Safety Commission estimated the cost of workplace stress, depression and anxiety to be in excess of £530 million.

References

1 Winton, W.M. (1987) Do introductory textbooks present the Yerkes–Dodson Law correctly? *American Psychologist*, 42, 202–203.
2 Yerkes, R.M., and Dodson, J.D. (1908) The relation of strength of stimulus to rapidity of habit-formation. *Journal of Comparative Neurology and Psychology*, 18, 459–482.

3   Britton, W.B. (2005) The physiology of stress and depression and reversal by meditative techniques. Presentation given at the Fourth Annual Conference for Clinicians, Researchers and Educators. Worcester, MA, 1–4 April. (3-hour DVD available.)

4   Csíkszentmihályi, M. (1991) *Flow: The Psychology of Optimal Experience*, HarperCollins, New York.

5   Oshry, B. (2007) *Seeing Systems: Unlocking the Mysteries of Organizational Life*, Berret-Koehler Publishers, San Francisco.

6   Selye, H. (1975) Confusion and controversy in the stress field. *Journal of Human Stress*, 1, 37–44.

7   Fryer, B. (2005) Are you working too hard? A conversation with Herbert Benson, http://hbr.org/2005/11/are-you-working-too-hard/ar/1 (accessed 2 March 2011).

8   Cited in Williams, M., Teasdale, J., Segal, S., and Kabat-Zinn, J. (2007) *The Mindful Way through Depression: Freeing Yourself from Chronic Unhappiness*, Guilford Press, London.

9   For a fuller discussion of the cycle of sacrifice and renewal see Boyatzis, R., and McKee, A. (2005) *Resonant Leadership*, Harvard Business School Press, Boston.

4

Approach and Avoidance
Learning New Ways to Be with
What Is

We don't altogether know why mindfulness training has the benefits that it does, and perhaps we can never know the whole story. But mindfulness is coming to be recognized as a highly effective way of training the mind and, as a result, is attracting increasing interest from neuroscience researchers.

A fascinating chapter in the story of the encounter between mindfulness and neuroscience began in 1992, when a small group of neuroscientists assisted by a Western Buddhist scholar journeyed up to Dharamsala in the foothills of the Indian Himalayas with an array of what was then cutting-edge scientific equipment: laptops, electroencephalographs, battery packs and a generator. Their aim was to meet some of the Tibetan Buddhist hermit-meditators who lived in the hills above the town, and to recruit a cohort of expert meditators

The Mindful Workplace: Developing Resilient Individuals and Resonant Organizations with MBSR, First Edition. M. Chaskalson.

from among them. They were looking for people who had put in tens of thousands of hours of meditation practice, and wanted to study the pattern of the hermit-meditators' brain activity. They weren't interested in whether the *state* they entered in meditation would be changed by that activity – that would obviously be the case. Rather they were interested in their *traits* – the habits of thinking and feeling they exhibited when *not* meditating. If they exhibited unusual traits, these would reflect enduring functional changes that had occurred in the brain as a result of their mental training.[1]

Initially the hermits weren't all that interested but, eventually, with the Dalai Lama's encouragement, 10 senior meditators enrolled in the study. For comparison, the scientists intended to study a number of ordinary Tibetans in the town, many of whom had fled Tibet around the time of the Dalai Lama's own escape in 1959. This first foray was doomed to failure. To begin with, the yogis were unimpressed by the scientists' materialist, apparently reductionist, perspective on meditation. 'We seemed like primitive Neanderthals to them', explained Alan Wallace, the Buddhist scholar who helped to facilitate the encounters. 'They thought, "What are you people measuring anyway, since you don't know the EEG correlate of compassion, or loving-kindness, or anything else?"'[1] (p. 218)

There were also clashes of culture. As an image meant to evoke contentment, whose neural correlate they wanted to measure, the scientists had chosen a wide landscape of dunes under a clear sunny sky. But the image made the yogi who was chosen to sit that test sad rather than contented. He imagined the suffering of someone who had to cross that bleak, broiling landscape. The image of a cute rabbit similarly misfired. Rather than evoking a sense of contentment, it made him wonder anxiously who would protect such a weak animal from predators.

In the end the scientists got no usable data from that trip. But they'd made a start and, with the Dalai Lama's help, in 2001 a number of maroon-robed Tibetan Buddhist monks began to make their way to Professor Richard Davidson's Laboratory for Affective Neuroscience in Madison, Wisconsin, to meditate in an fMRI scanner or have EEG caps stuck on their already shaven heads. These were 'Olympic-level athletes' of meditation, with between 15 and 40 years of intensive practice behind them.

The Dalai Lama's interest in the project had been piqued when he visited Davidson's lab for himself. He had his own question for the scientists: can the EEG and fMRI machines tell if a thought appears before changes arise in the brain? Does consciousness *precede* electrical or chemical activity? If so, then we might conclude that it is the mind that is acting on the brain and not just that the brain gives rise to the mind.[1 (p. 219)] This question is an intriguing one and it is still unresolved – perhaps the causal arrow runs two ways, with the mind being both the expression and the cause of physical changes in the brain. Whatever one makes of that question, the results that began to emerge from Davidson's laboratory are astonishing.

Davidson's earlier research emerged from clinical observations, made in the 1970s, that physical damage to one or another side of the prefrontal cortex – a small part of the brain just behind the forehead – had very different consequences on people's moods depending on whether the damage was to the left side or to the right. Damage to the left side caused people to be unable to feel joy. They sometimes also experienced acute increases in sadness accompanied by uncontrollable crying. In contrast, if the damage was to the right side, people were often indifferent to the injury and sometimes prone to inappropriate laughter. Digging deeper into the possible meaning of these findings, Davidson and his colleagues[2] reported that activity in the prefrontal cortex, as detected by EEG, reflects a person's emotional state and the extent of activation on the right or the left corresponds to a person's 'affective style'. When activity in the left prefrontal cortex is markedly and chronically higher than in the right, people are energized, alert, enthusiastic and joyful. They enjoy life more and have a greater sense of overall well-being. By contrast, when there is greater activity in the right prefrontal cortex, people report experiences of worry, anxiety and sadness. They are more discontented and rarely experience elation or joy. At the extreme, this indicates a high risk of clinical depression.

Ever since the 1970s researchers in the field of happiness and well-being have posited the idea of a happiness 'set-point'. The classic text on this goes back to 1971 when Brickman and Campbell argued that people are confined to a 'hedonic treadmill'.[3] By the time we become adults, they suggested, we experience more or less stable levels of well-being because, over time, we adapt to even the most extreme positive and negative life circumstances. If you're disposed to unhappiness, for example, and you win the lottery, you may cheer up for a time but you soon snap back and just become a grumpy rich person. On the other hand, if you're disposed to happiness and you lose an arm, you might grow unhappy for a time but, eventually, you're most likely to become a cheerful one-armed person.

Davidson was interested in the relationship between mental training exercises, such as meditation, and the happiness set-point. Could it be that, by altering the signals that the cognitive part of the brain transmits to the emotional part, you could, in an enduring way, change the pattern of prefrontal activation in a way that resulted in more frequent and more positive emotions? If scientists found again and again that people were returning to their happiness set-point, was it because they were studying people who, just like almost everyone else in the West, did not realize that you can build and change the brain's emotional circuitry in much the same way as you can build and change your biceps in a gym? Maybe no one had tried an intervention that shifted affective style in an enduring way. Davidson suspected that the happiness set-point was movable. The question was: what moved it?[1] (p. 231) This question is what led the steady trickle of maroon-robed monks to pass through his laboratory.

The results that emerged from these studies were extreme. To begin with, when they were meditating, the monks showed higher levels of gamma signals than had ever been recorded in a neuroscience study before.[4] Gamma-wave levels reflect the activation and recruitment of neural resources – mental effort. They appear when the brain brings together a number of disparate sensory features such as sound, look and feel and other attributes that lead to an 'aha!' moment of recognition – 'Oh yes . . . those white dots on the horizon . . . that's an offshore wind farm, not a flotilla of yachts!' Usually these signals last for a couple of hundred milliseconds. But in the adepts they lasted for up to five minutes. 'It was like a continuous *aha!* moment', said Davidson.[1] (p. 235) Mental training allowed the monks to produce heightened brain states associated with perception and problem-solving more or less at will while they were meditating. But even when they were not meditating they showed higher gamma activity. This hinted at what Davidson and others had been seeking in their initial trek into the Himalayas – evidence that mental training could produce enduring brain traits. This idea was strengthened when it became apparent that the more hours of meditation training the adepts had put in, the greater and more enduring the gamma signals they produced.

Other experiments, this time using fMRI, also produced unusual results, but one factor stood out from all the rest. While the monks were meditating, activity in their left prefrontal cortex swamped activity in their right prefrontal to an extent never before recorded. Left prefrontal activation is associated with happiness; right prefrontal activation is associated with negative moods such as unhappiness and with states such as anxious vigilance. These results suggested that emotions could be transformed by mental training. Perhaps the happiness set-point wasn't a set-point after all.

It's one thing to investigate the brains of really skilled meditators, quite another to see if those changes can be replicated in an ordinary population group. Davidson set out to conduct such a study in collaboration with Jon Kabat-Zinn, founder of the Mindfulness-Based Stress Reduction Clinic at the University of Massachusetts Medical School. As we have already seen, Kabat-Zinn and his colleagues teach mindfulness-meditation skills to patients with acute stress or chronic pain to help them better handle their symptoms. In an article published in *Psychosomatic Medicine* in 2003,[5] Davidson and Kabat-Zinn reported the effects of training in mindfulness meditation to workers in Promega – a high-pressure biotech business in Madison, Wisconsin. One group undertook an eight-week course in mindfulness training. A comparison group of volunteers from the company received the training later, and, like the participants on the first course, were tested before and after training by Davidson and his colleagues. Before the course, the whole Promega group – as with many who work in high-pressure environments – was tipped on average towards the right in the ratio for the emotional set-point and complained of feeling highly stressed. The group who received the mindfulness training, however, reported afterwards that their moods had improved. They felt more engaged in their work, more energized and less anxious. This was borne out by their brain-scan results. Their left-to-right prefrontal cortex activation ratio had shifted significantly leftwards. These results persisted at the four-month follow-up.

The subjective experience of participants complemented the objective data: meditation ultimately left people feeling healthier, more positive and less stressed. 'I really am an empiricist in every aspect of my life', said Michael Slater, a molecular biologist at Promega.

> I doubt dogma, and I test it. I do it at the laboratory bench, but also in my personal life. So this appealed to me, because I could feel the reduction in stress. I could tell I was less irritable. I had more capacity to take on more stressors. My wife felt I was easier to be around. So there were tangible impacts. For an empiricist, that was enough.[6]

Mindfulness also improved the robustness of the Promega meditators' immune systems. Both the meditator and the non-meditator groups were given flu jabs. Participants in the meditator group produced significantly more flu antibodies in their blood after receiving the jab. The greater the leftward shift in the emotional set-point, the larger the increase in the immune measure.

Eight weeks of mindfulness training in the workplace produced a more robust immune system in participants. It also significantly increased their left prefrontal-cortex activation and made them happier and less stressed. What is also really interesting from the workplace perspective is that it probably made them more innovative, more easily able to come up with creative solutions to problems. The idea that innovation and creativity are associated with happiness and well-being sounds intuitively obvious. Thanks to Davidson and others, however, we now know something of neuroscience that underpins that observation – and we might therefore be more readily able to train for these factors. There can be real productivity and creativity gains in doing so, for there is intriguing experimental evidence linking creativity to left prefrontal-cortex activation.

The story here goes back in evolutionary terms to the emergence of two distinct neurological processes: approach systems and avoidance systems. Writing in the 1970s and 1980s, Jeffrey Gray[7] proposed that two general motivational systems underlie behaviour and affect: a behavioural inhibition system (BIS) and a behavioural activation system (BAS). For simplicity's sake we might call these the *approach system* (for BAS) and the *avoidance system* (for BIS).

The approach system causes us to be sensitive to potential rewards and motivated to seek those rewards. Our sense of being attracted to a person or to a chocolate cake, as well as our desire to approach the person or the cake, emerges from this system. The avoidance system, on the other hand, sensitizes us to potential punishment or danger and motivates us to avoid it. That we may be fearful of rejection by someone we love, or be afraid of snakes, together with our desire to avoid such things, arises from the avoidance system. Davidson has shown that the approach system correlates to left prefrontal cortex activation.[8] It is reward-seeking and is associated with positive emotions such as hope and joy, as well as with the anticipation of good events. The avoidance system, on the other hand, which correlates to right prefrontal cortex activation, inhibits our movement towards goals and is responsive to cues of punishment or danger. It is associated with feelings of fear, anxiety and disgust.

It's easy to see the evolutionary value of these systems. They play a key part in the way in which you approach things you think will be good for you and avoid things that threaten you. But genetic and environmental factors can skew these mechanisms so that, as an adult human being, you may find, at one extreme, you have developed a chronically overactive avoidance system – leading you to be overanxious and prone to clinical depression. Mindfulness training, as Davidson and others[9] have shown, can change that. It can help you become more approach-oriented – and that, as we shall see, has an effect on your level of creativity.

In a study published in 2001, Ronald Friedman and Jens Forster[10] examined how the approach and avoidance systems affect creativity. They set two groups of college students a simple task. Both groups were given a sheet of paper which showed a cartoon mouse trapped inside a picture of a maze. The task was to help the mouse find a way out of the maze. But there was one slight difference in the pictures the groups received. The 'approach' version of the picture showed a piece of Swiss cheese lying outside the maze in front of a mouse hole. The 'avoidance' version showed an identical maze except that, instead of a satisfying meal of cheese at the end, an owl hovered over the maze – ready to swoop and catch the mouse at any moment.

The maze takes about two minutes to complete and all the students who took part solved it in about that time, irrespective of the picture they were working on. You might therefore think that there was no significant difference between the groups. But the difference in the *after-effects* of working on the puzzle was striking. When the participants took a test of creativity soon afterwards, those who had helped the mouse avoid the owl came out with scores 50% lower than those who had helped the mouse find the cheese. The state of mind that was brought about by attending to the owl had produced a lingering sense of caution, avoidance and vigilance for things going wrong. Those participants were comparatively more right-prefrontal-cortex activated. This weakened their creativity, closed down options for them and reduced their flexibility when it came to the creativity task. An increased left prefrontal cortex activation is associated with higher levels of creativity. By raising resilience it is also a predictor of more general well-being. Davidson defines resilience as 'the maintenance of high levels of positive affect and well-being in the face of adversity. It is not that resilient individuals never experience negative affect, but rather that the negative affect does not persist.'[11]

In an article published in 2004, Heather Urry and her colleagues[12] made the crucial distinction between eudaimonic and hedonic forms of well-being. Hedonic well-being focuses on issues such as life satisfaction, frequent pleasant emotions and infrequent unpleasant ones. Eudaimonic well-being, on the other hand, includes experiences such as a sense of autonomy, mastery of your environment, positive relationships, personal growth, self-acceptance, and meaning and purpose in life. Eudaimonia is associated with a deep sense of equanimity, of being at ease with yourself and your world, whereas hedonia is more about sensory pleasure. Using these two constructs, Urry and her colleagues showed that increased left prefrontal cortex activation involved more than just positive feelings. The approach-based mindset enables individuals to move towards events in their lives that create meaning and pleasure – and that certainly contributes to higher levels of well-being, but it also enables them to move towards distressful events with equanimity.[13] This ability to move towards uncomfortable experiences, rather than withdraw, is a description of resilience. It is also a key skill learned in the context of the MBSR course.

Time and again on the course the instructor will ask participants how they have experienced a practice they have just done. One of the key tasks here is to engage the participants in a curious, open, kindly and acceptant investigation of their immediate experience. In this way, they learn to approach, rather than avoid, challenging experiences in the moment – bringing an attitude of warm, kindly curiosity to whatever arises. In particular, participants learn to investigate the physical component of difficult experiences. It's not always easy to see at first what the value of doing this might be. It can seem so counter-intuitive. I had my own 'aha!' moment in this area several years ago when I was just completing the dissertation for my masters degree in the clinical applications of mindfulness.

In those days I tried to go away for a month each year and spend my time in solitude, meditating. I had arranged to rent an isolated cottage in the foothills of the French Pyrenees and the owner of the cottage was going to meet me at Carcassonne airport the next morning and drive me there. He was going to take me shopping for two weeks' worth of food en route to the cottage and a friend of his was going to bring me another two weeks' worth of food halfway through my retreat. This all seemed fine and I had a number of pressing tasks to complete before leaving the next morning. Before close of business that day I had to get the final draft of my dissertation off to my supervisor; I had to contact a number of clients and potential clients of my new mindfulness-training business; and I had to clear up many of the loose ends that come to mind when you're about to go away and be entirely out of contact for a month.

And then I had a sudden realization. Normally when I travel in France I use my debit card to withdraw the cash I need from an ATM machine as the need arises. For everything else, I pay with a credit card. But the owner of the cottage didn't take cards, nor did his friend, and at the airport I had to give him more euros for rent and food than the ATM machines would allow me to withdraw. I had to get some cash, and fast. Checking my watch, I saw I could do it – just – if everything went smoothly. I jumped on my bicycle, pedalled to the HSBC on Market Square in Cambridge, and stood in the queue at the bureau de change. There were two Dutch girls ahead of me in the queue. When they reached the cashier, they showed her the ATM machine they'd been trying to use in the bank.

'We have a problem', they said. 'Our ATM card doesn't seem to work here.'

'I'm sorry to hear that', said the cashier, 'but there's nothing I can do about that here. You'll need to contact your bank in Holland.'

'No, you don't understand', they replied. 'Our ATM card isn't working. It's a real problem. We're running out of money . . . '

'I *am* sorry to hear that', the cashier replied. 'But really, there's nothing I can do about it here. You'll need to contact your bank in Holland.'

'No, no, no!' they replied. 'You don't understand – our ATM card isn't working . . . '

And so the conversation ran.

Meanwhile, I was standing in the queue and feeling my temperature starting to rise. Precious seconds were flying by. I started to catastrophize.

'Oh no! I won't get my dissertation in on time. I'll miss my deadline. I'll not get my degree in time for the start of my new business. That's going to sink my credibility! My clients – I said I'd get in touch. No way will I be able to do that now. I'll never get any business from them. My reputation's going to go down the pan! My whole life, my plans and dreams, I'll never make it now . . . '

And so on. My jaw started to clench, my stomach tightened, my heart was racing . . . and I was about to intervene in the impasse in a rude way when a thought suddenly popped into my mind.

Michael! What's going on here? Come on – you're meant to be a mindfulness instructor!

Oh . . . right, so what are we meant to do here . . . ? OK, just pause, check in . . . What am I feeling here? Where am I feeling it?

'I'm hot! In my chest . . . It's really hot in there. It's like a kettle there – wow, it's steaming. There's a really hot spot, just below my chest bone, it's like there's a volcano! OK, so where aren't I feeling that? Well, there's nothing around my ribs, it's fine around there . . . '

In no time at all my inner landscape entirely changed. I moved from being stressed, anxious and about to be rude, to being curious and accepting – at least around my own experience. I moved from an avoidance mode of mind into an approach one and suddenly I was more resourceful – grounded and in the moment. The catastrophic scripts I'd been running just stopped and I was ready to deal effectively with whatever came next. As this happened the cashier, perhaps because she no longer had this Shrek-like figure looming over her customers' shoulders, about to pounce, resolved the situation quite quickly. I got my euros, did what I needed to do, went to France the next morning and had a productive retreat. It was an excellent lesson – acceptance and mindful curiosity have a real power to shift your mode of mind.

Try this:

The Physical Barometer

My colleague Trish Bartley at the Centre for Mindfulness Research and Practice at Bangor University has developed a practice called the 'Physical Barometer', which is designed to bring a heightened awareness of feelings into your everyday life.

If you have a barometer or have ever seen someone consult one, you will know that first you tap gently on the glass and then you look to see which way the needle inside the glass moves. If the needle moves up, the air pressure is rising and the weather will probably improve, and if the needle goes down, it may be going to rain. But things vary according to seasons, so it is quite complicated to predict the weather. We can use our bodies in a similar way to give us very sensitive information about how things are for us, at any given moment. Here is how you can do this:

1. Determine some part of the body – such as the chest area or the abdomen or somewhere in between the two – that for you is especially sensitive to stress and difficulty.
2. Once you have located this place it can become your 'physical barometer', and you can tune in to it, paying attention to sensations there regularly, at different moments, every day. If you are stressed, you may notice sensations of tension or discomfort. Depending on the intensity of the difficulty, these

sensations may be strong or not so strong and may change as you pay attention to them. If you are experiencing ease and pleasure and then tune in, you may notice quite different sensations.

3. As you become more practised at reading your physical barometer, you may find that you start to notice subtle variations that offer you detailed and early information about how you are feeling moment by moment, long before you are aware of this in your mind.

4. Any time you tune in to your physical barometer, if you wish, you can move to doing a mindful minute (see Chapter 3) to help you stay present with a difficult situation or with discomfort. Alternately, you may choose just to monitor the sensations in your physical barometer moment by moment and be with them just as they are. Just allowing things to be. Accepting, as best you can, how things actually are and being with your changing experience, from moment to moment.

References

1 Begley, S. (2007) *Train Your Mind, Change Your Brain: How a New Science Reveals Our Extraordinary Potential to Transform Ourselves*, Ballantine Books, New York.

2 Tomarken, A.J., Davidson, R.J., Wheeler, R.E., and Doss, R.C. (1992) Individual differences in anterior brain asymmetry and fundamental dimensions of emotion. *Journal of Personality and Social Psychology*, 62 (4), 676–687.

3 Brickman, P., and Campbell, D.T. (1971) Hedonic relativism and planning the good society, in *Adaptation-Level Theory* (ed. M.H. Appley), Academic Press, New York, pp. 287–305.

4 Lutz, A., Greischar, L.L., Rawlings, N.B., *et al.* (2004) Long-term meditators self-induce high-amplitude gamma synchrony during mental practice. *Proceedings of the National Academy of Sciences*, 101 (46), 16369–16373.

5 Davidson, R.J., Kabat-Zinn, J., Schumacher, J., *et al.* (2003) Alterations in brain and immune function produced by mindfulness meditation. *Psychosomatic Medicine*, 65, 564–570.

6 Stephen S. Hall (2003) Is Buddhism good for your health? *New York Times* (14 September), http://www.nytimes.com/2003/09/14/magazine/is-buddhism-good-for-your-health.html (accessed 8 March 2011).

7 Gray, J.A. (1981) A critique of Eysenck's theory of personality, in *A Model for Personality* (ed. H.J. Eysenck), Springer-Verlag, Berlin, pp. 246–276.

8 Davidson, R.J. (2003) Darwin and the neural bases of emotion and affective style. *Annals of the New York Academy of Sciences*, 1000, 316–336.

9 Segal, Z.V., Williams, J.M.G., and Teasdale, J.D. (2002) *Mindfulness-Based Cognitive Therapy for Depression: A New Approach to Preventing Relapse*, Guilford Press, London.

10 Friedman, R.S., and Forster, J. (2001) The effects of promotion and prevention cues on creativity. *Journal of Personality and Social Psychology*, 81 (6), 1001–1013.

11 Davidson, R.J. (2000) Affective style, psychopathology and resilience: Brain mechanisms and plasticity. *American Psychologist*, 1196–1214.

12 Urry, H., Nitschke, J.B., Dolski, I., *et al.* (2004) Making a life worth living: The neural correlates of well-being. *Psychological Science*, 15 (6), 367–372.

13 Siegel, D.J. (2007) *The Mindful Brain: Reflection and Attunement in the Cultivation of Well-Being*, W.W. Norton & Company, New York.

5

Metacognition
Knowing Your Thoughts as Thoughts

It is remarkable how liberating it feels to be able to see that your thoughts are just thoughts, and that they are not 'you' or 'reality' . . . the simple act of recognizing your thoughts as thoughts can free you from the distorted reality they often create and allow for more clear-sightedness and a greater sense of manageability in your life.[1] (pp. 69–70)

Jane leads a small team in a local-authority social-services department. Things have been really stressful for her. There have been deep cutbacks and more are coming. She and her team are being pressed to do more with less and she's spent weeks recently with her head down ploughing through data as she prepares for the annual review. She wants to be seeing clients, and to be available to her team, but there is so much

The Mindful Workplace: Developing Resilient Individuals and Resonant Organizations with MBSR, First Edition. M. Chaskalson.
© 2011 John Wiley & Sons, Ltd. Published 2011 by John Wiley & Sons, Ltd.

to do. She's had several late nights now, bringing figures up to date – ticking endless boxes to show compliance with a range of policies that, in her view, have no practical bearing whatever on the crucial service she and her colleagues provide. Despite the cutbacks, the number of clients being referred to them this month has significantly increased; staff members have been off sick or on their summer holidays and she is falling badly behind. Returning to her desk, having very briefly popped out to buy a lunchtime sandwich, she picks up a voicemail from Sarah, her line manager.

'Jane, we need to talk. Can you make 6 p.m. in my office?'

Another late night. But there's something else. Jane thinks she might have heard a slightly censorious tone in Sarah's message. She knows she's falling behind and she also knows the cutbacks have to fall somewhere. Immediately her mind runs to thoughts of redundancy. She feels a hollow feeling spreading from the pit of her stomach. She and her husband have just extended their mortgage to pay for a long-desired extension at home. It's taken them right to the edge of their capacity. She begins to feel nauseous as her imagination conjures up visions of the future: having to sell up and move, just as the children have settled in at school, maybe even eventual repossession. How would they cope without a home? Her parents have got limited room . . . and the chances of getting a new job in the current climate are really slim . . .

Struggling to put those thoughts from her mind, she feels herself getting more and more upset as her anger with Sarah (doesn't she know how hard she's been working?) begins to turn to something blacker. No one here really cares, she thinks, in the end you're on your own. Will they even remember her a few weeks after she's left? Fighting to contain her tears, she clenches her jaw, puts her head down and tries, unsuccessfully, to make progress with her figures. But all the time she's ruminating – why do things get to her like this? How come she's never really appreciated? What can she do about that?

Sarah's brief message sparked off a whole avalanche of feelings, thoughts and bodily sensations. But it's not just Sarah's tone that leaves Jane so incapacitated. Rather, it's as if a whole mode of mind – a pattern of negative thoughts, images, feelings and bodily sensations – has wheeled into place in response to Sarah's voicemail. This mode of mind includes both the negative thoughts, feelings and bodily sensations *and* Jane's tendency to try and deal with that by ruminating.

People like Jane spend a good deal of their time ruminating about why they feel the way they do – trying in that way to understand their own problems and inadequacies. They do so believing that this way of thinking will help them find ways to reduce their distress. But in reality this way of going about things is counterproductive. In states of low mood, repeatedly 'thinking about' negative aspects of yourself or your situation serves to perpetuate, rather than to resolve, your problem.[2]

By developing a mindful perspective on them, participants in mindfulness courses learn to see their thoughts just as thoughts, rather than as a reflection of reality or truth. This leads to reduced reactivity and lower levels of suffering and distress.[3-4] It also increases psychological flexibility – the ability to keep on with mental and physical behaviours that support what you want in your life and to avoid those behaviours that don't.[5] The benefits to be had from taking a mindful perspective on thoughts are considerable. Segal and colleagues,[6] for example, suggest that it interrupts the ruminative patterns of thought – such as those in the example of Jane above – that characterize many forms of distress. Teasdale and colleagues[7] suggest that mindfulness training has the capacity to bring about a state of 'metacognitive awareness' in which, rather than simply *being* your emotions, identifying personally with negative thoughts and feelings, you learn to relate to negative experiences as mental events in a wider context or field of awareness. That frees you from the distorted reality they create and can be hugely liberating.

But metacognitive awareness is not only helpful in respect of the negative or self-critical thoughts and feelings that accompany depression and other forms of distress. It can increase freedom and sense of choice in all aspects of your life. Take the case of Peter, who attended an MBSR course because he had had a heart attack and wanted to prevent another one. Peter came to a dramatic realization one night as he found himself, at 10 p.m., standing in his driveway washing his car under floodlights. He suddenly saw that he didn't need to be doing that. He had spent that day, as he usually did, determinedly trying to fit in all that he thought he needed to do. It struck him, in that moment, that he'd been unable to question the truth of his conviction that everything had to get done *today*. He was completely caught up in believing it and so, inevitably, he acted from that conviction. Washing the car was on his to-do list. If something was on the list, it had to get done. That attitude, Peter saw in a flash, was what led to his anxious sense of being constantly driven, his perpetual tension and his unconsciously anxious approach to life. That small, simple assumption gave rise to a set of attitudes and behaviours that threatened his heart and his health. As a result of his mindfulness training, Peter became more aware of his mental patterns. He saw that the thought 'I've *got to* wash the car next, it's on my list . . . ' was just a thought. He didn't *have* to do it. He could choose whether to continue or whether to stop and relax a bit before going to bed. He decided to call it quits.[1]

Participants on a mindfulness course learn metacognitive skills indirectly but very effectively. They may be instructed, for example, to meditate on their breath – simply allowing their attention to settle on the sensations of breathing. At some point during that meditation the instructor might suggest that when the mind wanders the participants should notice where it goes and then gently and kindly bring their attention back to the breath. At another point, he or she might add, 'And if your mind wanders off a hundred times, just bring it back a hundred times . . . ' The mind wanders, you notice where it went and you bring it back. It wanders, you notice where it went and you bring it back. Over and over. In this way, participants learn four key metacognitive skills:[i]

1. The skill of seeing that their minds are not where they want them to be.
    'I want to sit in this meditation, following my breath, but I keep thinking about what's next on my to-do list.'
2. The skill of detaching the mind from where you don't want it to be:
    'Actually, I don't need to be thinking about my to-do list right now: I can choose . . . '
3. The skill of placing the mind where you want it to be:
    'I'll just come back to the breath . . . '
4. The skill of keeping the mind where you want it to be:
    The participant just follows the breath for a few minutes, undistractedly.

By practising these four skills over and over, participants become more adept at them. That starts to have benefits outside of the meditation context as well: 'I don't need to be thinking about which holiday to book online when I get home – I need to give all of my attention to the client I've come to see'; 'Maybe I just *think* that my team leader has it in for me. Perhaps I need to check rather than take it as true.' Such enhanced attentional flexibility has considerable pay-offs in terms of increased performance at work – we all need to be able to focus better at times. But there is a greater freedom on offer as well. The repeated practice of these four skills can lead in time to what Teasdale calls 'metacognitive insight'.[4]

To illustrate the specific meaning of the term 'insight' here, Teasdale recounts the case of a recovered depressed patient attending a relapse-prevention programme. On the course, she developed the liberating metacognitive insight that 'thoughts aren't fact'. When she excitedly shared this insight with her husband, he responded saying 'I was born knowing that.'[4] From his perspective, the metacognitive *knowledge* that thoughts are not facts is simply commonplace. Yet, in that form, it had had little 'saving' power in protecting his wife from the effects of depressive thought patterns. The metacognitive *insight* she acquired through mindfulness practice, however, was one of the most important outcomes contributing to her continued good health.

To illustrate this point, Teasdale uses a traditional Sufi teaching story:

> Uwais was asked 'How do you feel?' He replied 'Like one who has risen in the morning and does not know whether he will be dead in the evening'. His questioner responded 'But this is the situation of all men'. Uwais replied 'Yes, but how many of them feel it?'[8] (p. 122)

There is a significant difference between the factual knowledge that we all may die at any time and the direct, experiential awareness, from one moment to the next, of that fact. The former is simply information whereas the latter can have pro-

found effects on our view of everything, radically transforming the way we live from moment to moment.

Human beings make meaning. That may be one of the
defining characteristics of our species. As Bertrand Russell
put it: 'No matter how eloquently a dog may bark, he cannot
tell you that his parents were poor but honest.'[9] But the meanings we make and the conclusions we can so quickly jump to
don't always fit the facts.

> John was on his way to school.
> He was worried about the maths lesson.
> He was not sure he could control the class today.
> It wasn't part of a janitor's duty.[6 (p. 244)]

Notice how you updated the scenario in your mind's eye as
you read from one line to the next. This is what we do all the
time – we very rapidly make meaning out of limited sensory
input and we constantly update that meaning as new data
becomes available. We create an ever-changing running commentary on the events that take place within our awareness.
Sometimes we get it wrong. This can lead to all sorts of problems because, often, along with these inferences come emotional reactions. Praise from a subordinate, for example, can
be read as 'he appreciates me' or 'he's sucking up to me' and
the reaction that follows will differ accordingly.

Even an identical event is liable to different interpreta-
tions. A manager and one of her staff are discussing certain
options:

'Would you prefer to attend the conference or stay and
catch up on your backlog?' the manager asks.

'I don't mind', her subordinate replies.

When the manager recounts this conversation to her own
line manager she remembers the event as: 'I asked him whether

he'd like to go to the conference or not and he said he didn't care.' Her subordinate, by contrast, recalls it as: 'She asked me whether I'd like to go to the conference or to stay and catch up and I said I didn't mind which – I'd just wanted to do whatever she thought would be most useful.' Separating events from the interpretation of events isn't always easy.

Consider some common mental habits:

- mind-reading: 'He thinks I'm stupid/boring/unattractive.'
- crystal-ball gazing: 'I'm not going to enjoy this.'
- over-estimating the negative: 'This is going to be a total disaster.'
- eternalizing: 'I'll never manage this/I'll always feel like this.'
- expecting perfection: 'I/people shouldn't ever make mistakes.'
- over-generalizing: 'This is difficult – everything's such an effort.'
- judgementalism: 'I wasn't able to do that – I'm just not good enough.'
- taking the blame: 'When things go wrong, it's my fault.'
- blaming: 'When things go wrong it's other people's fault.'

One can seek to address these tendencies explicitly – seeking evidence for or against their truth – or, as the MBSR course does, one can address them implicitly. Rather than dealing with individual unhelpful thoughts, the MBSR programme helps participants to recognize their thoughts *as thoughts* and to discover new ways of dealing with those that are unhelpful. The upshot of this is not only that they can find new ways of dealing with distressing thoughts, but also that they may become more flexible in their approach – more able to sit with difficulty and consequently more creative.

Valuable though it may be to recognize thoughts as thoughts, that is not the whole story. You might recognize the pattern of negative thoughts – see them for what they are – but beneath them, at a deeper level of the mind, there is going to be a set of feelings that gave rise to the thoughts in the first place. Such feelings often persist on the edge of awareness long after the thoughts that arose from them have passed out of awareness.[10] Taking this into account, the following exercise describes a routine for dealing with unhelpful patterns of thought.

Try this:

Working with Unhelpful Thoughts

When you find yourself caught up in unhelpful patterns of thought, try doing a mindful minute to gain some calm and steadiness. Then:

1. Acknowledge the thoughts for what they are. It may be helpful to put a label on them. 'There I go running my self-critical tape again', or 'Here I go judging others again', or 'Planning, I'm just doing my usual, anxious, over-planning . . . ' Just sit for a moment or two, gently acknowledging what's going on at the level of thoughts.
2. Now turn your attention to your body and see what's there at the level of feelings. Check out your directly sensed bodily experience. Maybe there's a slight feeling of anger present, or maybe sadness, anxiety or any other feeling. Just acknowledge whatever is

present at the level of feelings. And if there's not much going on there, just be aware of that.

3. Now see what's present in physical sensation. Maybe your shoulders feel tense or your jaw is clenching. Perhaps there's a tightening in your hands or across your brow. Again, just gently acknowledge what's there, bringing an attitude of warm, kindly curiosity to what you find. And sit with those sensations for a few moments, exploring them, breathing with them, just letting them be.

The simple act of becoming mindful of what is going on in thoughts, feelings and body sensations can create a deeper, more rounded quality of metacognitive awareness. By changing your relationship to what is present you're no longer driven unconsciously by it. That opens up more choice in your life and a greater possibility for a creative response to whatever is going on.

'People who cultivate mindfulness', says Annie McKee, founder of the Teleos Leadership Institute, 'improve cognitive flexibility, creativity, and problem-solving skills.' By learning to pay attention to the whole self – mind, body, heart and spirit – you can be quicker, smarter, happier and more effective than those who focus too narrowly or only on short-term success.[11]

Note

i   I am grateful for this rendering of the traditional Buddhist teaching of the Four Right Efforts to Dr John Dunne and his presentation on 'Mindfulness & Buddhist contemplative theory' at the 2007 Conference at UMass: 'Integrating mindfulness-based approaches & interventions into medicine, health care, and society'.

References

1 Kabat-Zinn, J. (1991) *Full Catastrophe Living: Using the Wisdom of Your Body and Mind to Face Stress, Pain and Illness*, Delta, New York.
2 Nolen-Hoeksema, S. (1991) Responses to depression and their effects on the duration of depressive episodes. *Journal of Abnormal Psychology*, 100, 569–582.
3 Baer, R.A. (2003) Mindfulness training as a clinical intervention: A conceptual and empirical review. *Clinical Psychology: Science and Practice*, 10 (2), 125–143.
4 Teasdale, J.D. (1999) Metacognition, mindfulness and the modification of mood disorders. *Clinical Psychology and Psychotherapy*, 6, 146–155.
5 Hayes, S. (2004) Acceptance and commitment therapy and the new behaviour therapies: Mindfulness, acceptance and relationship, in *Mindfulness and Acceptance: Expanding the Cognitive-Behavioral Tradition* (ed. S.C. Hayes, V.M. Follette and M.M. Linehan), Guilford Press, New York, pp. 1–29.
6 Segal, Z.V., Williams, J.M.G., and Teasdale, J.D. (2002) *Mindfulness-Based Cognitive Therapy for Depression: A New Approach to Preventing Relapse*, Guilford Press, London.
7 Teasdale, J.D., Moore, R.G., Hayhurst, H., *et al.* (2002) Metacognitive awareness and prevention of relapse in depression: Empirical evidence. *Journal of Consulting Clinical Psychology*, 70 (2), 275–287.
8 Shah, I. (1974) *Thinkers of the East*, Penguin, Harmondsworth.
9 Widdowson, H.G. (2003) *Linguistics*, Oxford University Press, Oxford, p. 5.

10 Williams, M., Teasdale, J., Segal, S., and Kabat-Zinn, J. (2007) *The Mindful Way through Depression: Freeing Yourself from Chronic Unhappiness*, Guilford Press, London.

11 McKee, A., Tilin, F., and Mason, D. (2009) Coaching from the inside: Building an internal group of emotionally intelligent coaches. *International Coaching Psychology Review*, 4 (1), 59–70.

6

Respond
Learning Not to React

Seeing your thoughts just as thoughts can open up new possibilities, new ways of being with the things that happen in your life. But not everything we react to comes to us as a result of our thoughts. We often react to things without thinking. In fact, we're hardwired to do so.

It's 4.30 p.m. and John sits at his desk, planning a presentation he's been asked to make to a key client in two days' time. While doing that, he's intermittently reminding himself to turn left at the lights on his journey home, not go straight on, as he usually does, because his wife has asked him to pick up her prescription from the pharmacy. Then John's manager drops by. He's just heard that the client needs that presentation tomorrow. John tries to say that it just can't be done – he won't have access to some key data before then and, in any

The Mindful Workplace: Developing Resilient Individuals and Resonant Organizations with MBSR, First Edition. M. Chaskalson.
© 2011 John Wiley & Sons, Ltd. Published 2011 by John Wiley & Sons, Ltd.

case, there's still so much to do. But John's manager is adamant. 'It's not my call', he says, 'it's out of my hands. It just has to be done by 2 p.m. tomorrow.'

As the conversation goes on its quality changes and John starts to feel bullied. There's a tone of pent-up frustration in his manager's voice that really disturbs him. His heart starts to pound and his hands grow moist. Trying to come back to planning the presentation after that, his thoughts are disorganized and he can't concentrate. However much he tries to stay focused, he just can't. He makes mistake after mistake. Arriving home late, the memory of the conversation with his manager stays with him as he berates himself for forgetting to stop at the pharmacy.

In response to acute stress, John became distracted and disorganized. His working-memory abilities worsened and habitual reactions took over his behaviour. John's amygdala and his sympathetic nervous system became activated. That caused him to remember the stressful event (and it allowed him to react more quickly) but his prefrontal cortex shut down and he became cognitively disabled in all kinds of ways.[1]

In evolutionary terms, when life was physically more precarious, as we've seen, this stress reaction produced the faster, habitual or instinctual behaviour necessary for survival. Enduring memories of stressful events enabled us to avoid such events in the future. But today these reactions can often be maladaptive. These days we're more likely to need prefrontal cortex regulation to act appropriately. When it comes to workplace stressors, we're not about to be eaten by tigers or speared by an enemy clan. Under modern conditions we actually need to keep thinking clearly and creatively to deal with the stressors that come our way. The trouble is, in the current work environment, we're often 'frazzled': overcome by the constant stream of daily hassles that switch our brains into crisis mode.

When you're frazzled, thought control shifts from the prefrontal area to the more primitive emotional circuitry of the midbrain and your system is set to give priority to speed over thoughtfulness and knee-jerk responses over creativity. The emotional centres of the brain then trump the prefrontal area, paralyzing your attention and reducing the space available in memory to take in new information and learn. The more you're frazzled, the less able you are to hold information in working memory, to pay attention or to react flexibly – let alone creatively.[2]

Mindfulness training can help to calm the amygdala.[3] How does it do that? Sitting on a train one day, on your way to work, you suddenly hear a shriek behind you from the opposite side of the carriage. Your back is towards the source of the scream and you face towards a man who immediately begins to look slightly anxious. Instantly, your cognitive capacities race to understand what has happened and what – if anything – you should do. Is it a fight? Is someone running amok on the train? Is danger approaching? Or was it perhaps just a shriek of delight – a group of teenagers having a good time? Your answer comes from the face of the man opposite who sees what is happening. His previously worried face now signals calm as he goes back to reading his newspaper. Whatever happened at the back of the carriage, you know that all is well.[4]

We are wired to react to changes in others. Their smiles, grimaces, frowns and grins give us a sense of how to interpret the signs of danger that sometimes signal another's intentions.[5] You can see the survival value of this. In the prehistory of our species, when we roamed the plains or jungles, a primal band that had many eyes and ears acting in combination would be much more vigilant than an isolated individual. In that world of tooth and claw, the ability rapidly – and sometimes silently – to pick up danger signals from all the available sentinels, as well as the capacity very quickly to mobilize each individual's fear response, significantly raised the odds of survival. This capacity for 'emotional contagion' – the finely honed human capacity for a person or a group to influence the emotions or behaviour of others through the conscious or unconscious induction of emotional states and behavioural attitudes – plays a significant part in the internal dynamics of any group.[6]

Because of the way we're wired we don't even need to be able to 'see' in the conventional sense for our eyes to pick up what is happening in others. A 52-year-old physician had suffered two strokes that damaged the connections between his eyes and the normal mechanisms for sight in his visual cortex. His eyes were intact and could take in signals but his brain couldn't decipher these or even note their arrival. To all intents and purposes he was completely blind. In tests where he was presented with a variety of abstract shapes such as circles and squares, or photographs of faces, he hadn't a clue what his eyes were registering. But when shown pictures of people with happy or angry faces he was able to guess which emotions were being expressed at a rate far better than could be attributed to mere chance.[7] So what was going on? Brain scans taken while this patient was guessing the feelings depicted on the photographs revealed an alternative to the usual paths that transmit data from the eyes to the thalamus – where sense information first enters the brain – and then to the visual cortex. This second route sends information directly from the thalamus to the amygdala, bypassing areas such as the visual cortex. The amygdala (we have two, one on the right, one on the left) then derives emotional meaning from that data – a frown, a change in posture, a shift in tone of voice – microseconds before we even know what it is we're looking at or hearing. What is more, there is no wiring from the amygdala to our centres for speech. When the amygdala registers a feeling, instead of alerting the verbal areas where words can express what we know, it causes the body to mimic the emotion in itself. The patient in question wasn't 'seeing' the images presented. He was feeling them, in his own body. This condition is known to researchers as 'affective blindsight'.

What this reveals is that there are two ways of processing emotion. Goleman[7] refers to these as a 'high road' and a 'low road'. The low road is made up of circuitry that operates below the level of our awareness and processes information very rapidly. Most of what we do, particularly in our emotional life, is driven by the massive neural networks that make up the low road. When you sense the sarcasm underlying a particular tone of voice, for example, or cheer up in response to a smile, that's the low road at work. The 'high road', on the other hand, comprises neural systems that work more methodically, step by step. We're aware of what is happening when we process things at this level and here we have some degree of control over our own inner life – a degree of control which is denied us at the level of the low road. When we think up a witty riposte to that sarcastic remark, or work out a way of getting closer to the person who smiled at us, that's all taking place via the high road. These two roads register events at different speeds. The low road is faster but less accurate; the high road, while slower, allows for a more precise view of what is going on.[8]

As we have seen, information that comes via the low road is often non-verbal, bypassing the speech centres. We feel it, whatever it is, but we don't say it. This 'gut feeling' can be quite literally that. We sometimes become aware of information communicated by the amygdala through circuitry that extends from it into the gastrointestinal tract.[9] Mindfulness practice can help you to tune in more accurately to this level of emotional processing, enabling you to manage your emotions better. Such self-management is crucial in the workplace, especially when it comes to dealing with the negative emotional surges – fear, anxiety, rage, frustration – that can sometimes be overwhelming. Goleman has coined the term 'amygdala hijack'[10] to describe what can happen to us in the grip of a negative emotional surge when the amygdala is suddenly activated and a variety of neurophysiological processes kick in so that activity in the low road swamps activity in the high road.

Two police officers were called to what seemed to be a domestic incident by a neighbour who was concerned about screams coming from the house next door. As they arrived, a terrified six-year-old boy ran out into the garden. Rushing to the living room, they found a panic-stricken woman being threatened by a man with a kitchen knife. The younger of the two officers was petrified. He'd never had to face an armed man before. He turned to his partner to see what he should do but his partner had frozen – he was the victim of an amygdala hijack and a sudden surge of adrenalin had stopped him in his tracks. He was in the grip of the body's 'fight, flight, freeze' response. Fortunately, the younger policeman's prefrontal lobes kicked in at this point. He realized that what he was seeing in the eyes of the man wielding the knife was actually fear. 'Are you OK, sir?' he asked. Immediately, the anger drained out of the man with the knife and he began to cry.[11]

What happened here was that, in a moment, the younger police officer acknowledged his own feelings and his inexperience, but he wasn't overwhelmed by them. He was able, instinctively, to regulate his own emotions. The capacity for non-reactivity under stress, self-composure and level-headedness shown by the younger police officer is one of the known outcomes of mindfulness practice.[12] Emotion is a complex phenomenon. It is a central, dynamic function that integrates behaviour, meaning, thinking, perceiving, feeling, relating and remembering. In terms of neurological activity, it includes processes that take place on both the high road and the low road. Mindfulness practice helps to develop emotional non-reactivity by developing those circuits of the brain that enable the lower, affect-generating circuits to be regulated by the higher, modulating ones. It beneficially alters the connections between the (low road) subcortical limbic amygdala and the (high road) prefrontal cortex.[13]

On a mindfulness course you learn, through practice, to identify and to 'let go of' passing emotional events. In meditation, for example, where the task is simply to follow the breath from moment to moment, your mind will naturally wander off that task. In the context of this approach, that's not seen to be a mistake or a fault. It's just what minds do. But when it happens you're encouraged to notice where your mind goes and perhaps to label that: 'Here's anger', for example, or 'Here's planning', and then just come back to the breath. In this way, you gradually become more acute at simply noticing what's present. You also become better at finding words for your experience.

Research by Creswell and colleagues[3] suggests that this enhanced capacity to find words for emotions as you experience them promotes a more effective recognition of such experiences. It allows you to detach from them to some extent, and to regulate your response more adaptively. The act of labelling emotions activates the prefrontal cortex and turns down activity in the amygdala. The integrative effects of mindfulness training allow the 'higher' prefrontal areas of the brain to coordinate and balance the activity in the 'lower', limbic areas of the brain. Put more simply, mindfulness training lets the smarter parts of the brain make more of the important executive decisions.

I meet frazzled people all the time in the organizations I work with and in the public courses I run. These are people who report, in the early part of a course, that they're unable to get their mind off their to-do list or the dozens of other work-related issues they're preoccupied with. In the early part of the course they'll often arrive late, dashing to take their seat and speaking of traffic hold-ups or unexpected events at home. They'll shuffle through the meditations and complain of never quite finding the time to do all of the home practice – there's just too much on in every part of their lives. There's a sense, in their jumpiness, that they're on a hair trigger for perceived threat or any other challenge. They often misread instructions in the handouts, forget which week of home practice we're meant to be doing, and don't manage to remember what time they're meant to return from a break. One of the many joys of the work is seeing people like this gradually begin to find some ease of being as the course progresses.

Frazzle and reactivity is enormously wasteful. It produces inefficiencies, mistakes and endless needless hassle. The cost of these to organizations is immense. Mindfulness training reduces reactivity. By learning to notice and find words for what is happening in your moment-to-moment experience you're able more effectively to regulate your emotional responses. As a result you'll be less likely to find yourself hijacked by the amygdala and less likely to become frazzled.

Try this:

Dealing with Frazzle

Next time you find yourself frazzled, overwhelmed by hassles and unable to stay focused, take a few minutes out.

Sit down somewhere where you won't be disturbed for three or four minutes (the lavatory will do if there's nowhere else) and just acknowledge what's going on. You're frazzled. Take a moment just to sit with that.

Then, bring your attention to the breath and do a mindful-minute meditation (see Chapter 3). Just follow your breath for however many breaths you normally take in a minute.

When you've done that, and maybe gained a little more calm and focus, turn your attention again to what's going on for you right now. What's the predominant emotion, if any? What's here, in your experience, right now? Try finding a simple label for that, without thinking too deeply about it. 'I'm angry', or 'I'm panicky', or 'I'm feeling overwhelmed' . . . Whatever it is, just acknowledge it and let it be.

Now take another mindful minute. Maybe things will have moved on.

References

1 Arnsten, A.F.T. (1998) The biology of being frazzled. *Science*, 280 (5370), 1711–1712.
2 Goleman, D. (2006) Aiming for the brain's sweet spot, http://opinionator.blogs.nytimes.com/2006/12/27/aiming-for-the-brains-sweet-spot/ (accessed 4 March 2011).

3   Creswell, J.D., Way, B.M., Eisenberger, N.I., and Lieberman, M.D. (2007) Neural correlates of dispositional mindfulness during affect labeling. *Psychosomatic Medicine*, 69 (6), 560–565.

4   Adapted from Goleman, D. (2007) *Social Intelligence: The New Science of Human Relationships*, Arrow Books, London.

5   Brooks, G., and Kulik, J. (1997) Stress, affiliation and emotional contagion. *Journal of Personality and Social Psychology*, 72, 305–319.

6   Barsade, S.G. (2002) The ripple effect: Emotional contagion and its influence on group behavior. *Administrative Science Quarterly*, 47, 644–675.

7   Cited in Pegna, A.J., Khateb, A., Lazeyras, F., and Seghier, M.L. (2005) Discriminating emotional faces without primary visual cortices involves the right amygdala. *Nature Neuroscience*, 8 (1), 24–25.

8   Williams, M.A., Morris, A.P., McGlone, F., *et al.* (2004) Amygdala responses to fearful and happy facial expressions under conditions of binocular suppression. *The Journal of Neuroscience*, 24 (12), 2898–2904.

9   Damasio, A.R. (2006) *Descartes' Error: Emotion, Reason, and the Human Brain*, Vintage, London.

10 Goleman, D. (1996) *Emotional Intelligence: Why It Can Matter More than IQ*, Bloomsbury, London.

11 HayGroup (n.d.) Amygdala hijack: Why being clever isn't everything, http://www.professional-learning.com/EIAmygdalaHijack.pdf (accessed 8 March 2011).

12 Baer, R.A., Smith, G.T., Hopkins, J., *et al.* (2006) Using self-report assessment methods to explore facets of mindfulness. *Assessment*, 13 (1), 27–45.

13 Siegel, D.J. (2007) *The Mindful Brain: Reflection and Attunement in the Cultivation of Well-Being*, W.W. Norton & Company, New York.

7

Mindfulness and Emotional Intelligence
Positive Relationships at Work

'You're wrong. You're dead wrong, and I'll tell you why.' With those words and the debate that followed it, Karl Albrecht's colleague lost his company several million dollars' worth of business.[1] The person he was speaking to was a civilian technical expert working at a senior level for the US Department of Defense and Albrecht's colleague, let's call him Jack, was a young man with considerable technical knowledge but few social skills. This was their first meeting with the government expert. Their intention was to begin building a relationship that would enable them to acquaint the expert and his colleagues with the technical capabilities of Albrecht's firm. In that way, they hoped to create a competitive advantage as a business contractor for the Department of Defense.

The government expert voiced a strong, and perhaps unsupportable, opinion about the future prospects for a certain type

The Mindful Workplace: Developing Resilient Individuals and Resonant Organizations with MBSR, First Edition. M. Chaskalson.
© 2011 John Wiley & Sons, Ltd. Published 2011 by John Wiley & Sons, Ltd.

of technology. Jack, blind to the larger context for the conversation, couldn't let that act of technical blasphemy go unanswered. He had to set the government expert straight and they were soon engaged in a heated debate. Far from achieving the objective of building a basis for a mutually respectful relationship, Jack very quickly achieved the exact opposite. Before Albrecht was able to shift the discussion back to neutral ground, the damage had been done. They never succeeded in getting another meeting with the expert or any of his colleagues. Jack had abstract intelligence, the 'IQ' kind, in abundance. But he lacked emotional intelligence – and that may have cost their firm millions.

The term 'emotional intelligence' (EI) was popularized by the psychologist Daniel Goleman, whose book of the same name,[2] published in 1996, was an instant bestseller and continues to be a standard text. Goleman's model of emotional intelligence sees it as an array of competencies and skills that drive leadership performance. He proposes four main EI constructs:

1. self-awareness – the ability to read your own emotions and recognize their impact while using gut feelings to guide decisions;
2. self-management – involves controlling your emotions and impulses and adapting to changing circumstances;
3. social awareness – the ability to sense, understand and react to others' emotions while comprehending social networks;
4. relationship management – the ability to inspire, influence and develop others while managing conflict.

Goleman includes a set of particular emotional competencies within each construct of EI. These competencies aren't innate talents. Rather, they are learned capabilities that can be worked on and developed. This is a key point. If EI competencies can be worked on and developed, what is the most effective way of doing that? Mindfulness training can play a large part.

Emotional-intelligence capabilities matter hugely in the world of work. To get a sense of what it contributes to people's performance and effectiveness, Goleman and colleagues analyzed data from close to 500 competence models from global companies such as IBM, Lucent, PepsiCo, British Airways and Credit Suisse First Boston, as well as public-sector and health-care organizations, academic institutions and so on. They wanted to discover those personal capabilities that drove outstanding performance in the people working there. To do this, they grouped capabilities into three categories: technical skills, such as accounting or business planning; cognitive abilities, such as analytic reasoning; and traits showing emotional intelligence, such as self-awareness and relationship skills.[3]

The results of the analysis were remarkable. As one might expect, intellect was to some extent a driver of outstanding performance. But the higher the rank of those considered to be star performers, the greater their level of emotional intelligence. When the comparison matched star performers against average performers in senior leadership positions, around 85% of the difference in their profiles was attributable to emotional-intelligence factors rather than to purely cognitive abilities such as technical expertise.[4]

There is a huge bottom-line value to these competencies. A detailed study by Boyatzis and colleagues[5] examined partners' contributions to profit in a large accounting firm in relation to their levels of EI. As might be expected, those whose analytic capacities were strong added 50% more to annual profits than those who were weaker in that area. But the real value came from those who were more emotionally intelligent. Those who were stronger in self-management competencies added 78% more profit than partners who lacked those strengths. Those strong in social skills added 110% more than those who weren't, and those who were particularly strong in self-regulation added an enormous 390% more. In the latter case, at 1999 levels, their contribution to profits was on average $1,465,000 more per partner. Higher levels of self-regulation are known to be one of the outcomes of mindfulness training.[6-7] But it is not only at these stratospheric heights that EI makes a difference at work.

In a cross-sectional survey,[8] Li-Chuan Chu examined 351 full-time working adults employed by public and private enterprises in Taiwan. A total of 60% of these occupied non-management positions, while 40% were managers. What they had in common was that all of them meditated, although they had different levels of meditation experience. Those participants with greater meditation experience exhibited higher EI, less perceived stress and less negative mental health than those who had lower levels of meditation experience. The study went on to randomly divide 20 graduate students with no previous experience of meditation into a mindfulness-meditation group and a control group. It measured both groups for the same variables and found that those who completed the mindfulness training demonstrated significant improvements with respect to EI, perceived stress and mental health compared to the control group. Mindfulness training is an effective means of developing EI. Above all, perhaps, it significantly enhances your capacity for empathy and attunement.[9]

For almost all of the 2.6 million years of human history up until the advent of agriculture about 10,000 years ago, our ancestors lived in tribal bands typically no larger than 150 members.[10] Competing with others for scarce resources, avoiding predators, constantly searching for food, in that harsh environment those who were able to cooperate typically lived longer and left more offspring.[11] Those who were better at teamwork usually beat those whose teamwork was weak. They were more likely to survive and it is their genes we have mainly inherited.[12] The evolutionary processes that shaped our neurobiological mechanisms gave rise to neural networks that allow us to empathize with others. We have the capacity to read the inner states of others to an extraordinary extent – far more than any other species on the planet – and these capabilities are driven by three different neural systems. We have the capacity to sense – and to simulate within our own experience – other people's *actions*, their *emotions* and their *thoughts*.[13]

The networks in your brain that light up when you perform an action also light up when you see someone else perform it. That gives you, in your own body, a felt sense of what others experience in their bodies.[14] The way these networks 'mirror' the behaviour of others gives them their name: mirror neurons. When we see people choking up in distress, for example, we literally feel what they are feeling – although usually to a lesser extent – in our own bodies. Similarly, we experience some of the physical components of elation when we see people who have a sudden burst of happiness.

But there are affective, emotion-related circuits forming our experience as well. And the neural circuits that are active when you experience strong emotions, such as fear or anger, are sympathetically activated in you when you see others having the same feelings. The networks that produce your own feelings allow you to make sense of the feelings of others[15] and so the more aware you are of your own feelings and body sensations the better you will be at reading these in others.

Yet another set of circuits comes into play when you come to 'read' the thoughts and beliefs of other people. The prefrontal circuits involved in helping us to guess the thoughts of others, which only come to their full development quite late in life, possibly not before late adolescence, work in conjunction with the circuits involved in sensing the feelings and actions of others to produce your overall perception of their inner experience.[16] The more mindful you are – the better you are able to experience your own thoughts, feelings and body sensations – the better you will be able to accurately perceive the thoughts, feelings and body sensations of others.

The capacity to empathize more deeply with others is crucial in the world of work. Whether the other person is a customer, a client, a colleague, an employer or an employee, the capacity to be fully present to them and to demonstrate the sense that you see them as a person with their own individual thoughts and feelings is crucial to all vital relationships. This capacity for two people to 'feel felt'[9 (p. xiv)] by each other is a key factor in allowing those in relationship to one another to feel vibrant, alive, understood and at peace.

One context where we all feel the presence or absence of such attunement is in the doctor–patient relationship and that was the context for a workplace study that was carried out in Rochester, New York, in 2009. According to Michael Krasner, associate professor of clinical medicine at the University of Rochester Medical Center:

> From the patient's perspective, we hear all too often of dissatisfaction in the quality of presence from their physician. From the practitioner's perspective, the opportunity for deeper connection is all too often missed in the stressful, complex, and chaotic reality of medical practice.[17]

In a study published in the *Journal of the American Medical Association* in 2009,[18] Krasner and his colleagues reported the results of a mindfulness course they carried out with 70 primary-care doctors in Rochester. As other similar studies have shown,[19-20] the training significantly alleviated the psychological distress and burnout that is often experienced by many physicians and improved their well-being. But it also expanded their capacity to relate to patients and enhanced patient-centred care. Enhancing the capacity of the physician fully to experience the clinical encounter, in its pleasant and unpleasant aspects, non-judgementally and with a sense of curiosity and adventure, had a profound effect on the experience of stress and burnout. It also enhanced their ability to connect with each patient as a unique human being and to centre their care around that uniqueness.

Like many doctors, Edward Stehlik thought he was reasonably good at connecting with his patients and helping them manage their health. But he also sometimes found himself distracted by other demands – the insurance form he hadn't completed, a colleague's email that needed answering. 'There's no question', he said, 'especially after you've been in practice for a while, that there are times when you're not as engaged with patients as you should be.'[21] He signed up for the mindfulness course. 'If you asked my patients now', he said, 'I think they would say I listen more carefully since the training and that they feel they can explain things to me more forthrightly and more easily.' As with doctors, so with us all. The more mindful you are, the more empathic you will be and that is the *sine qua non* of all social effectiveness in working life.[4]

As we have seen, in order to connect effectively with others you need to have ready access to your own thoughts, feelings

117

and body sensations. But you also need to be in a certain quality of relationship to these. It's not easy to connect with others if you hate or dislike your own thoughts, feelings and body sensations, or if you are narcissistically bound up with them. Kristin Neff, who specializes in the study of self-compassion at the University of Texas at Austin, suggests that these tendencies are countered by the cultivation of self-compassion. Mindfulness training, she notes, has been shown to increase this.[22–24]

According to Neff, there are three main components to self-compassion:

1. self-kindness – being kind and understanding towards yourself when you experience pain or failure rather than being harshly self-critical;
2. common humanity – seeing your experiences as part of the larger human experience rather than as leading to separation and isolation;
3. mindfulness – the ability to hold painful thoughts and feelings in balanced awareness rather than over-identifying with them.

Self-compassion protects you against the negative consequences of self-judgement, isolation and depressive rumination. Because of its non-evaluative and interconnected nature, self-compassion counters the tendencies towards narcissism, self-centredness and downward social comparison that can be associated with other attempts to maintain self-esteem[23] – when you're mindful, you don't need to put others down. Self-compassion also naturally raises your level of concern for the well-being of others. It involves seeing your own experience in light of the common human experience. Here, you acknowledge that suffering, failure and inadequacy are part

118

of the human condition and that everyone – yourself included – is worthy of compassion. Being less judgemental towards yourself, you become less judgemental of others. This is because comparisons between yourself and others aren't needed to enhance or defend your self-esteem. Compassion isn't extended to yourself because you are superior or more deserving than others. Rather, it's felt because you recognize your interconnectedness and equality with the rest of humanity.[23] So a key element in the process of developing empathy is the cultivation of self-compassion which is a natural by-product of mindfulness training.[22]

Perhaps the most widely used mindfulness programme that focuses specifically on the cultivation of emotional intelligence is that run by Google at their headquarters in Mountain View, California. Entitled 'Search inside yourself', the programme was founded by Chade-Meng Tan, a long-time Google employee who was much taken with the evidence basis for MBSR. But for Meng, stress reduction wasn't enough.

> For high achievers, stress can be a badge of honour, and not many people will sign on for stress reduction, particularly those who need it the most. So I needed to go beyond stress reduction. I wanted to help people find ways to align mindfulness practice with what they want to achieve in life . . . [25]

To succeed at Google, among all those scientists and engineers, the mindfulness course had to be 'data-driven', but establishing that mindfulness practice was scientifically valid was just one element in a larger campaign. For it to be widely adopted, people needed to think of it as something as normal and as obviously beneficial as taking physical exercise. When people there started to see it as a workout for the heart and mind, it could become a part of the fabric of their daily lives. That was where emotional intelligence came in. It seemed like something that everyone would like to have and that would be appealing in a business context, as a means of making people more effective.

Google is a hugely successful business and, as in all companies, there needs to be a business justification for whatever is done there. Meng felt EI would appeal to engineers and high-achieving people because they can often have problems in dealing with difficult conversations. 'We either avoid them or go at them like rampaging geeks. Either way, we recognize it's a deficiency.' What is more, software engineers can sometimes think that the most important thing is coding. Interacting with others can take a back seat. But, as one gets into higher levels of engineering, according to Meng, at least half of the work is about talking to people. Learning to emerge from your shell and interact well is what emotional intelligence is all about. Besides mindfulness training, the course at Google looks at themes such as 'The neuroscience of empathy', and they frequently invite eminent guest speakers such as sleep scientist William Dement and neurobiologist Dan Siegel to contribute.

The first course ran from October to December in 2007 and it has been offered regularly ever since. By September 2009 more than two hundred people had gone through the program. One of the themes discussed on the Google course is mindful emailing. Participants are taught to take three breaths after typing an email, look again, imagine how the other person will receive it, imagine their mental and emotional response, and then alter the email if need be. One person came back the week after learning that and reported that he was amazed at how much of a difference it made when he was reflective about email:

I wrote this whole email out, and I knew it was really important for the person to receive it with openness to my ideas. But the message was emotionally loaded, so he might not respond very openly. I looked at it carefully and reflected, and then I did something very radical. I called him on the phone.

Others in the class nearly gasped, and then he said, 'You know, it really worked!'[25]

Try this:

Working with Empathy

Here are five steps to the mindful development of empathy you might experiment with.

1. Notice the behaviour of others.
    This is not about reading body language, rather it is about getting the mirroring functions in your own brain activated. By mindfully attending to the other person's stance, gestures and actions, the corresponding circuits in your own brain will become active. Perhaps even mimic some of the gestures, unobtrusively. See what that feels like. What does your body tell you then?
2. Tune in to your own feelings and sensations.
    Become aware of your own breath and settle into yourself. Tune into your own feelings and body sensations in the moment. This mindful attention to your own experience stimulates and primes those

121

parts of your brain that allow you to read the experience of others.

3. Watch the other person's face and eyes.

   Paul Ekman[26] has shown how our emotions – anger, fear, disgust, sadness, happiness and so on – cascade as expressions across our faces, providing clear signals to those who can identify the clues. These can take the form of micro-expressions that flit across the face and eyes and change very rapidly. With mindful attention you are better able to spot these and by consciously attending to the face and eyes you have a much better chance of reading them.

4. Attend to your own thoughts and actively imagine the thoughts of the other person.

   As you notice the other person's behaviour and begin to get a sense of their feelings and sensations, partly from reading your own, and as you watch their face, thoughts will begin to form in your own mind. Notice these and imagine as well what might be moving in a corresponding way in the mind of the other person. Since you have a natural capacity for empathy it is likely that your own thoughts will be in some ways aligned with the thoughts of the other person.

5. Check back and stay open.

   Thoughts aren't facts! Always check that what you think the other person is thinking and feeling is what they are actually thinking and feeling. Ask open questions and be ready to revise your opinion.

References

1 Albrecht, K. (2005) Social intelligence: The new science of success, https://www.karlalbrecht.com/articles/socialintelligence.shtml (accessed 4 March, 2011).

2 Goleman, D. (1998) *Working with Emotional Intelligence*, Bantam Books, New York.

3 Goleman, D. (2001) An EI-based theory of performance, in *The Emotionally Intelligent Workplace* (ed. C. Cherniss and D. Goleman), Jossey-Bass, San Francisco, pp. 27–44.

4 Goleman, D., Boyatzis, R., and McKee, A. (2004) *Primal Leadership: Learning to Lead with Emotional Intelligence*, Harvard Business School Press, Boston.

5 Boyatzis, R., Goleman, D., and Rhee, K. (2000) Clustering competencies in emotional intelligence: Insights from the emotional intelligence competence inventory, in *The Handbook of Emotional Intelligence* (ed. R. Bar-On and J.D. Parker), Jossey-Bass, San Francisco, pp. 343–362.

6 Shapiro, S.L., and Schwartz, G.E. (2000) Intentional systemic mindfulness: An integrative model for self-regulation and health. *Advances in Mind–Body Medicine*, 16 (2), 128–134.

7 Baer, R.A. (2003) Mindfulness training as a clinical intervention: A conceptual and empirical review. *Clinical Psychology: Science and Practice*, 10 (2), 125–143.

8 Chu, L.-C. (2010) The benefits of meditation vis-à-vis emotional intelligence, perceived stress and negative mental health. *Stress and Health*, 26, 169–180.

9 Siegel, D.J. (2007) *The Mindful Brain: Reflection and Attunement in the Cultivation of Well-Being*, W.W. Norton & Company, New York.

10 Norenzayan, A., and Shariff, A.F. (2008) The origin and evolution of religious prosociality. *Science*, 332, 58–62.

11 Wilson, E.O. (1999) *Consilience: The Unity of Knowledge*, Vintage, London.

12 Nowak, M. (2006) Five rules for the evolution of cooperation. *Science*, 314, 1560–1563.

13 Hanson, R., and Mendius, R. (2009) *Buddha's Brain: The Practical Neuroscience of Happiness, Love and Wisdom*, New Harbinger Publications, Oakland, CA.

14 Preston, S.D., and de Waal, F.B.M. (2002) Empathy: Its ultimate and proximate bases. *Behavioral and Brain Sciences*, 25, 1–72.

15 Singer, T., Seymour, B., O'Doherty, J., *et al.* (2004) Empathy for pain involves the affective but not sensory components of pain. *Science*, 303, 1157–1162.

16 Singer, T. (2006) The neuronal basis and ontogeny of empathy and mind reading: Review of literature and implications for future research. *Neuroscience and Biobehavioral Reviews*, 30, 855–863.

17 Science*Daily* (2009) Mindful meditation, shared dialogues reduce physician burnout, http://www.sciencedaily.com/releases/2009/09/090922162259.htm (accessed 4 March 2011).

18 Krasner, M.S., Epstein, R.M., Beckman, H., *et al.* (2009) Association of an educational program in mindful communication with burnout, empathy, and attitudes among primary care physicians. *Journal of the American Medical Association*, 302, 1284–1293.

19 Iacovides, A., Fountoulakis, K.N., Kaprinis, S., and Kaprinis, G. (2003) The relationship between job stress, burnout and clinical depression. *Journal of Affective Disorders*, 75, 209–221.

20 Oman, D., Richards, T.A., Hedberg, J., and Thoresen, C.E. (2008) Passage meditation improves caregiving self-efficacy among health professionals: A randomized trial and qualitative assessment. *Journal of Health Psychology*, 13 (8), 1119–1135.

21 Novotney, A. (2010) A prescription for empathy. *Monitor on Psychology*, 41 (1), 46.

22 Allen, M., Bromley, A., Kuyken, W., and Sonnenberg, S.J. (2009) Participants' experiences of mindfulness-based cognitive therapy: 'It changed me in just about every way possible'. *Behavioural and Cognitive Psychotherapy*, 37 (4), 413–430.

23 Neff, K. (2003) Self-compassion: An alternative conceptualization of a healthy attitude toward oneself. *Self and Identity*, 2, 85–101.

24 Shapiro, S., Brown, K.W., and Biegel, G.M. (2007) Teaching self-care to caregivers: Effects of mindfulness-based stress reduction on the mental health of therapists in training. *Training and Education in Professional Psychology*, 1 (2), 105–115.

25 Boyce, B. (2009) Google searches, http://shambhalasun.com/index.php?option=com_content&task=view&id=3417&Itemid=244 (accessed 4 March 2011).

26 Ekman, P. (2007) *Emotions Revealed: Recognizing faces and feelings to improve communication and emotional life*, Times Books, New York.

8

Mindfulness for Leaders

Some people seem to be born happy. Some seem born to be great leaders. How much of this is down to how the brain is wired – and how much of it can be changed?

As we saw earlier, since the early 1990s, neuroscientists have broadly accepted that people who show more activity in the left prefrontal cortex of their brains tend to feel that they have their lives under control. They experience a sense of personal growth, meaning and purpose. They have good personal relationships and accept themselves for who they are. They take what may be broadly characterized as an approach orientation to life. Those whose right prefrontal cortex is more activated, on the other hand, are by contrast more discontented and unhappier. They can feel that their lives are out of control and are perhaps disappointed with

The Mindful Workplace: Developing Resilient Individuals and Resonant Organizations with MBSR, First Edition. M. Chaskalson.

how things have turned out for them. Dissatisfied in their personal relationships and with their work, they rarely feel emotional highs. People at this end of the emotional spectrum are more avoidance-oriented.[1] Those who take an approach orientation to life are generally more effective leaders and the tendency to avoidance orientation, which is often a consequence of the stresses that leaders experience, can be reduced by mindfulness practice.

If you plot the ratio of left and right prefrontal cortex activation across a general population group you get a bell-curve distribution. Most people are in the middle part of that curve, experiencing a mixture of approach and avoidance attitudes, having a mix of good and bad moods, left and right prefrontal cortex activation. Those relatively few people who are furthest to the right will be most likely to experience a clinical depression or anxiety disorder over the course of their lives. Those very fortunate people furthest to the left rarely experience troubling moods and recover from them very quickly. Mindfulness training, as we saw in Chapter 4, can shift this ratio for individuals.[2] As evidenced in its capacity to increase the extent of left prefrontal activation, it can make you more approach-oriented. And that makes for better leadership.

You can't easily pin down the essence of good leadership but, if you've ever worked under a good leader, you'll know how satisfying that can be. Good leaders make work enjoyable, however demanding it is. They inspire their teams to give of their best, skilfully drawing on the talents and temperaments of their people. You could describe what they do as the creation of resonance[3] because they draw out and amplify the qualities of those around them. People who do this tend to be highly approach-oriented. They are curious, kind, open, compassionate, tolerant and accepting – all of these are approach-based emotions and will be associated with left prefrontal activation. Dissonant leaders, by contrast, drain the enthusiasm of teams and organizations. They lower morale and make those around them unhappy. They tend to be very avoidance-oriented and tend towards control, aversion, intolerance, irritability and fear.

Richard Boyatzis, professor of organizational behaviour at the Weatherhead School of Management, specializes in the study of leadership. Good leaders, he says, attain resonance with those around them through self-awareness, self-management, social awareness and relationship management,[3] all of these being, to some extent, mindfulness skills. But the demands of leadership produce 'power stress', a known side effect of being in a position of power and influence that often leaves even the best leaders physically and emotionally drained. As a result, leaders can easily find themselves moving from an approach orientation to their task – emotionally open, engaged and innovative – to an avoidance orientation that is characterized by aversion, irritability and close-mindedness.

Mindfulness training strengthens the tendency towards the approach mode of mind. It teaches you to take an interest in all aspects of your experience and to 'approach' it, treating it with acceptance and curiosity. A formal training in mindfulness skills gives you the tools to switch from an avoidant to an approach mode of mind. It teaches you to embrace and understand the entirety of each moment. Real mindfulness is imbued with warmth, care and curiosity. It consists in an engaged interest in whatever is before you, and where there is that kind of interest a kindly, natural and unforced attention follows.

The pressures that pull managers into dissonance are increasing. This is fed by a number of issues. Time compression, the flood of data, the demands of multitasking and the feeling that the world is increasingly unsafe are huge pulls towards dissonant experiences.[4] To be effective as a leader, you need to intentionally work towards maintaining resonant relationships with your people. Mindfulness training can help.

Take the case of Julia (not her real name), a leader I worked with in a professional-services firm. She is a successful partner in a thriving firm, who had 20 staff reporting to her. For one reason or another, she was beginning to find life at work a little cramping. It just wasn't as satisfying as it had once been. As a result she was growing tetchy and irritable, and – although she never blew up – she was often seen to be visibly working hard to control her temper. That made for a stressful working environment and the team's quality of work was affected. A 360° feedback assessment showed that her people were starting to find her intimidating, and that was affecting the quality of their work. One of the people responsible for HR in the firm suggested she might benefit from a few sessions of coaching. Julia agreed, maybe a little reluctantly. Time, after all, is what professional services is all about. When you bill in minutes there never seem to be many of those to spare. Nonetheless, Julia went along and she and her coach began to unearth the frustrations that underlay her irritability. The coach, who was trained in mindfulness, suggested to Julia that she might like to experiment with the mindful minute, mentioned in Chapter 3. Julia, who is nothing if not meticulous and conscientious, took that up and was surprised at how much of a difference it made – and how quickly. Intrigued, she signed up for an eight-week one-to-one mindfulness course. She now practises mindfulness on a daily basis, and she, her team and her family have all variously reported how much of a positive difference that has made. She now has the resources to deal much more effectively with what she'd previously found frustrating.

In *Becoming a Resonant Leader*, McKee and colleagues[5] outline three contemporary myths about leadership and suggest alternative truths. Myth One states that 'smart is good enough'. Obviously, they say, you have to be pretty intellectually sharp, talented and experienced if you're to lead a complex organization or social system. No one would succeed who didn't understand the numbers, the environment in which they operated, their stakeholders and their technology. But hundreds of studies have shown that the competencies related to emotional and social intelligence have a much greater impact on predicting leadership effectiveness.[6] Social intelligence determines how leaders understand and interact with others. Emotional intelligence informs how they deal with their own states of mind – their moods and emotional responses. Leaders with higher levels of social and emotional intelligence are more effective because they act in ways that leave their people feeling stronger and more capable. They manage themselves more effectively in the face of stress and ambiguity. Knowing at all times how their people are thinking and feeling, socially and emotionally intelligent leaders are able to motivate and inspire them. They create exciting, challenging and supportive environments that are able to generate and sustain long-term success.

Key to all of this, say McKee and her colleagues, is self-awareness. That is, the ability quickly and accurately to process emotional information, to recognize emotions as they happen and immediately to understand their effects on oneself and others. Good leaders know their own strengths as well as their limitations. Knowing their values and the principles they stand for, they believe in their own abilities and communicate a sense of self-assurance and effectiveness. This kind of self-awareness, the bedrock of emotional intelligence, provides a solid foundation for self-confidence.

A neurobiological study published by Creswell and colleagues in 2007[7] showed evidence that mindfulness training increased the level of emotional self-awareness. The ability to know and to articulate what you are feeling, they found, correlated strongly with the ability to manage the effects of negative feelings. This is an intriguing study because it shows that we all have the ability to improve our capacity to notice and interpret our emotions. But just knowing your own feelings isn't enough. To lead, you also need to manage your responses. As we saw in Chapter 3, we're biologically hard-wired always to react to apparent threats from the environment we're operating in. We react to organizational and psychological challenges as if our life depended on it. The exact same mechanisms that ensured the survival of our prehistoric ancestors when they were hunting on the plains and threatened by a predator are activated in us when we encounter an organizational threat at work. Adrenalin, noradrenalin and corticosteroids flood our system, raising our heart rate, pumping our large muscle groups with blood, shutting down our digestion and preparing our bodies to heal from bites or bruises.

But we usually don't get into those kinds of fights in the office and the effects of sympathetic nervous system over-stimulation are deeply harmful over time. The ability accurately to scan the working environment and to respond appropriately is a crucial key to success in the complex and stressful world of work today. But it's not easy, and studies have shown that one of the key obstacles to executive success in organizations is a lack of emotional self-control.[8] People who frequently lose their temper don't make good leaders – nor do those who freeze under pressure. Leaders whose emotions are out of control, or inappropriate, push people away. It is vital, therefore, that leaders are able to monitor their own emotional states and able to understand how they affect others. Leaders are being watched by their people all the time. Their power over others is a key component in the working environment and so their people judge their moods and try to predict their likes and dislikes, their desires and their likely behaviour. This leads to McKee and colleagues' second great myth of leadership today.

Myth Two states that 'mood doesn't matter'. As we saw in Chapter 6, emotions are contagious. We're wired constantly to tune in to the mood and the emotional state of the people around us, and that affects how we feel, what we think and what we do. The way people perceive their leaders' states has a direct effect on their well-being. Wager and her colleagues,[9] for example, measured a variety of physical responses, including blood pressure, on groups of employees who worked under supervisors, some of whom were perceived favourably, others unfavourably. Those who worked under unfavourably perceived supervisors exhibited markedly higher blood pressure and other physical signs of distress. When people are fearful, anxious or angry they move into an avoidant mode of being characterized by right prefrontal cortex activation and chronic sympathetic nervous system arousal. As a result they shut down, fight back or want to run away. Often, they feel frazzled and don't perform at their best. By contrast, when they are optimistic, energized and excited they think more clearly and creatively, are more resilient and perform better.

In two experiments carried out in 2005 with a group of 104 college students, Barbara Fredrickson and Christine Branigan[10] exposed their subjects to short film clips which elicited feelings of amusement, contentment, neutrality, anger and anxiety in turn. After each of these they measured the students' 'thought-action repertoires' – in other words the variety of thoughts they might have and the kinds of actions they might undertake in relation to these. What they found was that, when the students were experiencing negative feelings, they had a much narrower variety of thoughts and actions available to them. The thoughts and actions they reported under these circumstances were broadly in line with the ideas of attacking or fleeing. When they experienced positive emotions, on the other hand, they had a much wider range of options available to them. What is more, the negative experiences tended to narrow their scope of attention, whereas the positive ones tended to broaden that. Negative emotions lead to diminished creativity; moods do matter and, since leaders' moods are especially contagious, leaders' moods matter a lot. As we have seen, mindfulness training enables you to manage your moods much more effectively. People who have trained in mindfulness experience negative moods less frequently and, when they do experience them, they are better able to see what is happening and to take action to address that.

The third great myth of leadership that McKee and colleagues draw attention to is that 'great leaders can thrive on constant pressure'. In their work with leaders across a range of organizations around the world, McKee and her colleagues have noticed a growing problem. Even good leaders are struggling to maintain effectiveness in the face of the immense challenges they face every working day. Too many of them are slipping into destructive patterns of behaviour and they're taking their people with them.

The world in which leaders have to operate seems to be increasingly unstable. Economic, social and environmental instability is the norm. Technological change races ahead. At the personal level, the demands of work are relentless. Leaders are never unplugged from it. There are round-the-clock emails and calls, and leaders very rarely escape the demands of clients, customers, employees or other stakeholders. Their emotional resources are constantly being tapped and they are expected to give unceasingly.

Unending responsibilities, constant pressure and 24/7 availability can often lead to the experience of power stress. This is inherent in the leadership role and it can cause leaders to fall into what McKee and colleagues call the 'sacrifice syndrome' – a vicious cycle of stress and sacrifice that results in mental and physical distress, burnout and diminished effectiveness. And that spreads. Emotions are contagious and stressed leaders spread dissonance throughout their teams and organizations. With the best intentions leaders often find that they drive themselves and their teams onwards – striving to meet crucial deadlines, attend important meetings and presentations, go on business trips and so on – while all the time failing to notice they're gradually becoming less optimistic, less hopeful and more exclusively task focused. It doesn't take long down that spiral before they've lost their edge, soured their relationships and become less effective than they were in the heady earlier days of their leadership.

To counter the eroding demands of power stress and the sacrifice syndrome, McKee and colleagues suggest that leaders need to understand the crucial part that renewal plays in sustaining their effectiveness. They suggest there are three vital practices that leaders can engage in to stop the sacrifice syndrome before it stops them. These practices are mindfulness, hope and compassion. Mindfulness, they say, is a state of reflection and openness in which you are tuned in to yourself, others and your environment. This is brought about through deliberate mindfulness practices, which enable renewal by reconnecting leaders to those aspects of themselves and the rest of the world that inspire them and bring out their best qualities. Leaders need crucially to attend to their own needs if they are to remain effective, and mindfulness practices have been shown over and again to produce highly effective returns on the time invested in them. Hope, according to McKee and her colleagues, is what you feel when you look forward to a future that seems both feasible and enticing. It carries you through life's transitions and provides the energy and resilience to face the future with courage. Leaders who have hope in this sense inspire their people with a vision of where they might go together, providing them with a sense of purpose and direction. The sense that it's possible to achieve great things together makes for resonant relationships, bringing out the best in each person. Compassion, they say, is empathy in action. Leaders who care for their people, are willing to act in their best interests, and those who are seen to do so bring about the best in their teams. They inspire trust and confidence. People give more for leaders who they know have their best interests at heart. The resonance that flows from mindfulness, hope and compassion is a vital creative energy that supports higher productivity, more creativity, a sense of unity and purpose, and produces better results. When people are positively challenged, hopeful and enthusiastic, they tend to be more open, adaptable and creative.

These approach orientations have tangible results at work. Positive affect even allows people to process more information and to do so faster.[11] So not only does mindfulness training play a crucial role in enabling leaders to renew themselves, it also helps them to deal with the tendency to cognitive overload that is so much a part of the current work environment. When faced with complex problems, says Ben Bryant, professor of leadership and organization at IMD business school in Switzerland, people in organizations tend to multiply the sources and quantity of information available, and this frequently results in information overload. Leaders can become prisoners of too much cognitive input when what they should do is improve the quality of the attention they give to the here and now.[12] Mindfulness frees up mental energy and allows us to pay heed to immediate experience – as it happens. Bryant cites the case of a CEO of a major utility company who was sensing high levels of power struggle and resistance during a meeting with his executive team. This is a common enough phenomenon, at whatever level of an organization one works. After prolonged debate, it appeared that consensus had finally been reached on the issue of a recent takeover. But the CEO noticed that the dissonance hadn't really subsided and he sensed that there was still some emotional resistance under the surface. So he stopped speaking, looked around the table into each team member's eyes and sat down. 'OK', he said. 'Let's just drop this agenda today. What is really going on here, guys? How's everyone feeling right now?' The team members started to speak from their emotions, describing what was going on for them. Everyone became more aware of what was happening within themselves and for each other. The conversation, which had been stuck until that point, became more exploratory and creative.

The CEO's mindfulness heightened his sensitivity to his own and his team members' emotional discomfort. Instead of automatically closing the meeting after it looked as if they had achieved consensus, he unexpectedly stopped the discussions with a surprising question that invited everybody into the present moment. By detaching himself and his team from the meeting agenda, noticing his surroundings and becoming aware of the here and now, he allowed others to free themselves from the emotions and frustrations they had been holding. The meeting had technically finished, but he made the mindful choice to focus on detaching from what was *apparently* going on and focusing instead on what was *really* going on. The effect of this was liberating for everyone.[12]

Bill George, professor of management practice and Henry B. Arthur Fellow of Ethics at Harvard Business School, is an enthusiastic advocate of mindfulness in leadership contexts. In an interview published in Harvard Business School's online newsletter, *Working Knowledge*,[13] George described the 'Mindful Leadership Conference' he co-hosted in August 2010. This brought together 400 participants in an exploration of how mindfulness can contribute to sustaining effective leadership. For George, leaders who fail to develop self-awareness are often seduced by external rewards such as power, money and recognition. They find it hard to acknowledge their mistakes, and that has been an Achilles heel that has brought down a number of CEOs – many of these in high-profile cases in recent years. According to George, mindfulness can contribute very usefully to the self-awareness and self-compassion of leaders. Mindfulness, he says,

> is a state of being fully present, aware of oneself and other people, and sensitive to one's reactions to stressful situations. Leaders who are mindful tend to be more effective in understanding and relating to others, and motivating them toward shared goals.[13]

As a result, they become more effective leaders.

In George's view, leaders with low emotional intelligence can lack the self-awareness and self-compassion needed for self-regulation. That makes it very difficult for them to feel compassion and empathy for others and they struggle to create sustainable, authentic relationships. Not taking any time for introspection and reflection, such leaders also feel a need to appear so perfect to others that they don't admit their vulnerabilities or acknowledge their mistakes. He cites the recent difficulties at Hewlett-Packard, British Petroleum, the many recently failed Wall Street firms, and the dozens of leaders who failed in the post-Enron era. Much of that, he suggests, can be accounted for by a lack of self-awareness and self-compassion. By contrast, effective leaders demonstrate a kind of authenticity. They are genuine and true to their beliefs, values and principles. These qualities make up what he calls someone's 'True North'. Authenticity, he says, is developed by becoming more self-aware and by a kind of compassion for yourself. Without that, it's not really possible to feel genuine compassion for others.

In teaching authentic-leadership development and the idea of True North to students and seasoned leaders, George has learned that the greatest challenge comes when the pressures and seductions are most intense. That is when it is most important to be self-aware and that is where mindfulness plays a part. Mindfulness is a logical step in the process of gaining self-awareness and any business school or other training institution committed to developing leaders needs to offer courses and other experiential opportunities that enable students to develop greater awareness of themselves, their motivations, and their strengths and shortcomings.

Try this:

Tweaking Your Day

Leaders, we've seen, really need to take care of themselves to avoid falling into the sacrifice syndrome and spreading dissonance through their teams. But the responsibility to take care of ourselves begins with each of us individually – whether we lead or not.

Make an inventory of a typical working day. You might try making a list of all the things you do in a fairly average day, for example:

- wake up;
- first cup of tea;
- check the BlackBerry;
- check the news;
- breakfast;
- kids off to school;
- drive to work;
- and so on . . .

Then, being as frank as you can, ask yourself: 'What of all these things I do and take in actually nourishes me?' What energizes you, makes you feel calm and centred? What increases your sense of actually being alive and present, rather than merely existing? Put a plus (+) alongside these.

Then ask: 'Of these things that I do and take in, what depletes me?' What pulls you down, drains your energy, makes you feel tense and fragmented? What decreases your sense of actually being alive and present, what makes you feel you are merely existing, or worse? Put a minus (–) alongside these.

Then, consider those things that are neutral – that don't bring you up, and don't bring you down. You just do them as part of your routine. Put a slash (/) alongside these.

Finally, consider what gives you a sense of mastery. These are things that you might not find particularly pleasant – tidying a sock drawer or paying the backlog of household bills, for example – but when you've done them they leave you with a sense of accomplishment. You feel glad to have done them. Write M alongside these.

Now, accepting that there are some aspects of your life that you simply can't change, how can you consciously choose to increase the time and effort you give to the things that nourish you? How can you decrease the time and effort you give to the things that deplete you? And is there any way to change some of the neutrals into positives – to make them more nourishing and/or enjoyable?

Finally, can you learn to approach the things that at present you find depleting in a different way? Maybe by being more fully present with them, even if you find them boring or unpleasant – bringing the same curiosity and attention to them as you did to the raisin – instead of judging them or wishing that they were not there?

By being present in more of our moments, and making mindful decisions about what we really need at each of those moments, we can use activity, and the choices we make about what we take in, to become more aware and alert. This is true both for the regular pattern of our daily lives and for times of difficulty in our lives. We can use our day-by-day experience to discover and cultivate activities that nourish us, which we can use as tools to cope with periods of challenge. Having these tools already available means that we will be more likely to persist with them in the face of difficulty and of our habitual responses to these times.

For example, one of the simplest ways to take care of your physical and mental well-being is to take daily physical exercise – as a minimum, aim for three brisk 10-minute walks a day – and also, if at all possible, other types of exercise such as yoga, qigong, swimming, jogging and so on. Once exercise is part of your daily routine, it is readily available as a way of responding to external and internal difficulties as they arise. And, naturally, a regular mindfulness meditation practice will offset many of the negative demands of your day.

References

1 Begley, S. (2007) *Train Your Mind, Change Your Brain: How a New Science Reveals Our Extraordinary Potential to Transform Ourselves*, Ballantine Books, New York.

2 Davidson, R.J., Kabat-Zinn, J., Schumacher, J., *et al.* (2003) Alterations in brain and immune function produced by mindfulness meditation. *Psychosomatic Medicine*, 65, 564–570.

3 Boyatzis, R., and McKee, A. (2005) *Resonant Leadership*, Harvard Business School Press, Boston.

4 Boyatzis, R. (2005) Resonant leadership encourages leaders to work towards mindfulness, hope and compassion in relations with others, http://www.case.edu/news/2005/12-05/resonant. htm?nw_view=1299499973& (accessed 7 March 2011).

5 McKee, A., Boyatzis, R., and Johnston, F. (2008) *Becoming a Resonant Leader*, Harvard Business School Press, Boston.

6 Boyatzis, R. (1982) *The Competent Manager: A Model for Effective Performance*, Wiley & Sons, Inc., New York.

7   Creswell, J.D., Way, B.M., Eisenberger, N.I., and Lieberman, M.D. (2007) Neural correlates of dispositional mindfulness during affect labeling. *Psychosomatic Medicine*, 69 (6), 560–565.

8   McCall, M.W., Lombardo, M.M., and Morrison, A.M. (1988) *The Lessons of Experience: How Successful Executives Develop on the Job*, Free Press, New York.

9   Wager, N., Fieldman, G., and Hussey, T. (2003) The effect on ambulatory blood pressure of working under favourably and unfavourably perceived supervisors. *Occupational Environmental Medicine*, 60 (7), 468–474.

10 Fredrickson, B., and Branigan, C. (2005) Positive emotions broaden the scope of attention and thought-action repertoires. *Cognition and Emotion*, 19 (3), 313–332.

11 Forgas, J.P. (2003) Affective influences on attitudes and judgements, in *Handbook of Affective Sciences* (ed. R.J. Davidson, K.R. Sherer and H.H. Goldsmith), Oxford University Press, Oxford, pp. 596–618.

12 Bryant, B. (2008) Mindfulness. *Perspective for Managers*, 162, http://www.imd.ch/research/publications/upload/ PFM162_LR_Bryant_Wildi.pdf (accessed 7 March 2011).

13 Silverthorne, S. (2010) Mindful leadership: When East meets West – Q&A with: William W. George, http://hbswk.hbs.edu/ item/6482.html (accessed 7 March 2011).

9

Mindfulness in Coaching

One of the ways in which mindfulness is finding its way into workplace settings is through the coaching relationship. There are three broad dimensions to this. Coaches can use mindfulness to enhance and extend their coaching skills. They may recommend mindfulness training to their clients and, if they have the necessary skills and training, they can offer mindfulness interventions or exercises as part of their coaching programme.

In a study published in 2008,[1] the performance psychologist Gordon Spence presented evidence that clients who received mindfulness training prior to embarking on a course of cognitive-behavioural solution-focused coaching experienced higher levels of goal-directed self-regulation as a result of the coaching than a control group who did not receive the mindfulness training. That stands to reason. People who have learned, through mindfulness training, to be less reactive in

The Mindful Workplace: Developing Resilient Individuals and Resonant Organizations with MBSR, First Edition. M. Chaskalson.
© 2011 John Wiley & Sons, Ltd. Published 2011 by John Wiley & Sons, Ltd.

respect of their thoughts, feelings and body sensations, are likely to experience higher levels of mental and emotional flexibility. They are likely to feel that they have more choice and they will experience higher levels of metacognitive awareness. These qualities will all have a bearing on the outcome of their coaching.

There has, to my knowledge, not as yet been any significant research carried out into the impact of mindfulness training on coaches. But there has been useful work done on the impact of mindfulness in psychotherapy and one may perhaps legitimately read across from that. One of the more intriguing studies is that carried out by Grepmair and colleagues in Germany.[2] They conducted a randomized and double-blind controlled study that followed the therapeutic course and treatment results of a group of inpatients. There were 124 patients, treated for 9 weeks by 18 psychotherapists in training. Half of the psychotherapists practised mindfulness meditation and half did not. On examination, it turned out that the results of the therapy delivered were significantly higher on a range of evaluations for the clients of the therapists who practised mindfulness. Their clients also showed greater symptom reduction than the non-mindfulness-trained group. The study concluded that promoting mindfulness in psychotherapists in training could positively influence the therapeutic course and treatment results experienced by their patients. It seems very likely that similar results would show up if one carried out a similar study with coaches. All other things being equal, coaches who are trained in mindfulness will have several advantages over those who have not had such training.

In an article published in 2007 in *The Coaching Psychologist*,[3] Passmore and Marianetti conclude that a coach's practice can be enhanced through training in mindfulness in four distinct areas:

1. Preparing for coaching

   Whether they are self-employed and working with all the unpredictability that comes with that or whether they work within large organizations and experience the many and various large and small tensions that typically arise in such conditions, coaches experience stress in their working lives. In either case, like most people at work today, they have to deal with information overload and time stress. Whether struggling to stay on top of an email backlog or anxiously hurrying to make their next appointment on time, coaches who don't successfully manage their own stress will be less effective for their clients.

   Rushing from one meeting or coaching session to another, coaches can find that their own focus is sometimes more on ensuring they get to their sessions on time, or arrive at the right place, than allowing enough time to leave behind the thoughts, pressures and anxieties of the day. Mindfulness practice offers coaches a practical way of putting such demands aside and dealing with their various stressors. That lets them bring their attention much more fully to the needs of their client and to the session that is about to take place.

2. Maintaining focus in the session

   Mindfulness enables the coach to remain focused during the session. Mindfulness practice helps coaches to improve their focus and concentration in ways that have significant benefits during coaching sessions. Mindful coaches are able to maintain a kind of watchfulness over their own minds. They're better able to disengage from wandering thoughts and fantasies and to continually bring their attention back to the client when they notice their focus starting to drift.

3. Remaining emotionally detached

    Mindfulness helps coaches to manage their changing moods and emotions during the coaching session. Such emotional detachment is a key coaching skill. Coaches need to experience the emotions being felt by their client, but not be 'flooded' by them to the point where these emotions prevent the coach from helping the client to move forward.

    Flooding occurs when, for example, the coach finds themselves crying at the news of their client's dismissal, or when the coach overidentifies with the experiences of their client to the point where they themselves feel anger towards the client's boss or other adversary. Mindful coaches are able at such times to empathize with their clients while still being in a position to provide them with constructive challenges. The 'intimate detachment' of reperceiving that we discussed in Chapter 1 allows the coach to stand back a little from their own moment-by-moment experience and to be with their own distress in a more objective way. Being able to do that effectively for themselves, they are also able to do it effectively with their clients.

4. Teaching mindfulness to clients

    Coaches may also choose to teach mindfulness practices directly to their clients. It is crucially important, though, that coaches who choose to do this maintain their own personal mindfulness practice. They should certainly meditate every day. As Segal and colleagues[4] put it, a swimming instructor is not someone who knows the physics of how solids behave in liquids. Rather, he or she knows how to swim. Sharing their understanding of the brain's neuroplasticity and of the value of training the brain just as one trains the body, mindful coaches can invite their clients to imagine how the benefits of mindfulness might impact on them and their performance. As clients become more interested in these practices, coaches can introduce them to guided meditation CDs, and recommend books or mindfulness courses. They can share practices like the mindful minute and, if they feel confidently able to do that, longer practices as well.

But more importantly, perhaps, than these four areas, mindfulness helps the coach to empathize with their client. As we saw in Chapter 7, the more mindful you are – the better you are at reading your own thoughts, feelings and body sensations – the better you will be at accurately perceiving the thoughts, feelings and body sensations of others. Mindfulness enhances the coach's capacity to be fully present to their clients, to give them a sense that they are being fully heard and fully seen in a context where their unique experience as an individual is accepted and not judged. That allows the client to 'feel felt' by the coach and is a key factor in the transforming power of the coaching relationship.

The classic expression of the qualities that bring about effective change in a therapeutic or coaching relationship were first spoken of by Carl Rogers, working in the 1950s, who described three core conditions for therapeutic change.[5] The first of these could be called genuineness, realness or congruence. The more the therapist is simply himself or herself in the relationship, putting up no front or facade, the greater is the likelihood that the client will change in a constructive manner. This calls for the coach to be open to and accept the feelings and attitudes that are flowing within them in any moment. Mindfulness training significantly enhances a coach's ability to do this.

The second attitude that is important in creating a climate for change is acceptance – what Rogers called 'unconditional positive regard'. When the coach experiences a positive, acceptant attitude towards whatever the client is at that moment, change, according to Rogers, is more likely to occur. This calls on the coach to be willing for the client to be with, and simply to experience, whatever immediate feeling is going on for them – confusion, resentment, fear, anger, courage, love or pride. The attitudes of kindness, openness and acceptance are natural outcomes of mindfulness training.

The third of Rogers' core attitudes is empathic understanding. This involves the coach accurately sensing the feelings and personal meanings that the client is experiencing. The coach then communicates that understanding to the client. At its best, the coach becomes so attuned to the client's inner world that he or she can clarify not only the meanings of which the client is aware, but even those just below the level of awareness. That kind of sensitive, active listening is rare for many people. As Rogers put it: 'We think we listen, but very rarely do we listen with real understanding, true empathy. Yet listening, of this very special kind, is one of the most potent forces for change that I know.'[5 (pp. 115–116)] As we have seen, mindfulness training can significantly enhance the coach's capacity for empathy.

All the coaching associates at my company, Mindfulness Works Ltd, use mindfulness in one way or another in their coaching relationships. Each of them is a graduate of the Mindfulness for Coaches course that we run and each has found that mindfulness has made a significant difference to the way they coach. Bryan Emden, for example, a coach and supervisor at the Emden Partnership in London, considers that his own mindfulness training has allowed him to connect in a different way to the manner in which his clients communicate. He often draws clients' attention to the way they're breathing at the start of the session. 'That gives both of us valuable information about how they're feeling', he says. 'We might then go onto a short mindfulness exercise after which they often discover greater clarity of thought and observation. Clients often find then that they speak in a more reflective and a clearer way, with greater curiosity.' The clarity and objectivity that emerges from such dialogues allows Bryan's clients to observe their thoughts and feelings rather than being preoccupied by them – and that makes for much more effective coaching outcomes.

Emma Donaldson-Feilder, another of our coaching associates and director of Affinity Health at Work, uses mindfulness for herself as a coach and, where appropriate, to support her coaching clients with their development. Her clients often find that being more mindful helps them to achieve the outcomes they are looking for. Sophie, the chief executive of a medium-sized private-sector consultancy, was struggling with her leadership role during a time of rapid organizational change and came to coaching to explore how she could maintain her clarity of leadership vision despite the uncertainty with which she and her senior-management team were faced. Through coaching, Sophie was enabled to adopt a more mindful approach. Emma shared some mindfulness practices with her and gave her a CD to support her practice at home. This enabled her to deal better with some of the issues that troubled her at home. By being more present to, and more mindful of, the range of emotions she was handling both there and at work, she felt more able to be authentic and better placed to inspire her team.

Simon, a manager in a large IT company, was struggling to juggle the range of pressures presented by his role. He had recently been off sick with stress-related health problems and sought coaching on his return to work in order to prevent stress from further damaging his health. Emma taught him a number of mindfulness techniques that he used to help centre himself and focus on what he wanted to achieve. He learned to walk mindfully to and from the Tube station each day, and to pay particular attention to the experience of his morning shower. Conflict at work had been a particular challenge for Simon. When one of his colleagues disagreed with him, he found it hard to stay calm and would often become defensive or aggressive, which he generally regretted afterwards. As part of his coaching, Emma encouraged him to shift his attention to his breathing for a moment before responding in conflict situations. This moment of 'grounding' helped him refocus on what was important to him in that discussion and make better choices about how to respond.

Jane Brendgen, another of our coaching associates, thinks of mindfulness as a way of refining attention and cultivating an open-hearted presence. That, she sees, allows her to bring her whole self to the engagement with the client, being fully in the moment with *and for* the client, with little self-centred purpose in mind. 'Through inwardly attending to my own process in the moment with an accepting, non-judgmental attitude – touching my feelings, thoughts and intuitions – I use myself as an instrument to guide my responses to my client. That produces a much greater sense of true presence and deep listening', she says. This way of being places her directly in the here-and-now encounter with her client. Through attending to this, she is better able to stay attuned to her client's emerging needs and to play with 'negative capability' – the willingness to stay with uncertainties without reaching prematurely for a conclusion. This is where Jane finds she can meet and respond effectively to the central question in relational coaching – which of the whole range of things that she can do in any moment is the best for her client?

Emily came to coaching to address the slow pace of her career progression. She and Jane began by looking at the leadership competencies Emily needed to develop. Early on in their conversation, Jane became aware of feeling undermined and noticed that she was beginning to take on a defensive position. With presence of mind, she paused, grounded herself by using her mindfulness skills and, with her curiosity and non-judgemental attitude restored, moved from the countertransference position back into the present moment. The data this awareness provided, together with a strong intuitive sense, guided her line of questioning. The hypothesis that was forming was centred on the nature of Emily's relationships with her managers and stakeholders. Jane wondered whether they too might have felt undermined by her and she was interested in the obvious impact that might have had on Emily's career progression. In the next session Jane shared her own experience and the associated hypothesis with Emily. With further exploration, the conditions that triggered that pattern in Emily became clear and she realized that her tendency to undermine others was a significant feature of the relationships with her last three managers. With that expanded awareness she moved away from blaming her environment and started trying out a new way of being with her current manager. In addition, her relationship with Jane as her coach became more authentic and open.

Rosemary's manager enrolled her for coaching to support her with behavioural changes around defiance, anger and negativity. She was reluctant to engage with the coaching and Jane noticed the impact this had on the development of their working alliance. 'Initially I found it very difficult to connect with her', Jane said. One of the early coaching sessions was devoted to talking through feedback from Rosemary's managers. One piece of feedback triggered a powerful reaction in

Rosemary and she began to rage. 'In that moment', said Jane, 'I turned to my breath, felt my feet on the ground and was able to remain present – "holding" her with a kind and compassionate attention as she expressed those difficult and strong emotions. I was able to meet her with the same mindfulness and non-reactive calm acceptance with which I am learning to meet my own experience.' This had a significant effect on their relationship and enabled Rosemary to trust that Jane would not run from her anger. When they met at the next session Rosemary was open, warm and available to be coached.

In my own experience as a coach, I find that one of the most effective and transformative aspects of the coaching I offer comes from my own attempts to maintain an attitude of mindfulness before, after and during the coaching session. By holding open the space of mindfulness I engage my clients as fully as I can. Aware of my own thoughts, feelings and sensations in the moment, maintaining an attitude of allowing and acceptance, focusing closely on what is said and communicated by other means in the session, my clients can come to feel something of the quality of mindfulness for themselves. Sometimes they'll want to learn more about that. Sometimes simply being heard and responded to mindfully is all they need. Mindfulness can transform the coaching relationship.

Try this:

More Mindful Coaching

If you're a coach you'll be aware of how easy it is for your mind to wander in the middle of a coaching session. However interested you might be in your clients and their issues, sustaining continued attention on them for two hours or more is never easy. What is more, you need to be prepared for each session – not breathless after a rushed walk up from a station or taxi, nor with your mind full of the BlackBerry email you just received or the mobile phone call you just made.

On the Mindfulness for Coaches course we teach these simple techniques:

- Make this a ritual part of your practice. In the five minutes before you are due to arrive at the client's office (or they at yours), switch off your mobile phone and any other communications device and establish mindfulness. If you're still walking at this point, make it a mindful walk. If you're sitting, close your eyes and follow your breath for three to five minutes.
- During the coaching session, when you notice that your mind has wandered, notice where it went – that may have some bearing on the session, it may tell you something about how you're responding to your client. Then, bring your attention back – first of all to yourself. Perhaps designate some part of your body that will be your personal anchor point. This might be the sensation of touch and contact where your feet meet the floor, or it might be that sense of slight stretching in your belly as your breath comes in. Whenever you notice that your mind has wandered, bring your attention back to this anchor point and then very deliberately move it back to your client. Coming back to yourself first helps you to stay present. It allows you to be with your

client in a different way. If you don't first come back to yourself you can lose yourself either in your wandering mind or in the client's story. Neither of these is as helpful to the client as the sense they would otherwise get of your continual mindful presence.

- If the session becomes stormy and your client is angry or in any other way inflamed, keep your balance by bringing your own attention to your anchor point. Feel your breath, perhaps, or become aware of your feet on the floor. Maintaining your own equanimity and equilibrium while also being with your client may be the best gift you can offer them at such times.

References

1 Spence, G. (2008) *New Directions in Evidence-Based Coaching: Investigations into the Impact of Mindfulness Training on Goal Attainment and Well-Being*, VDM, Saarbrucken.

2 Grepmair, L., Mitterlehner, F., Loew, T., *et al.* (2007) Promoting mindfulness in psychotherapists in training influences the treatment results of their patients: A randomized, double-blind, controlled study. *Psychotherapy and Psychosomatics*, 76 (6), 332–338.

3 Passmore, J., and Marianetti, O. (2007) The role of mindfulness in coaching. *The Coaching Psychologist*, 3 (3), 131–138.

4 Segal, Z.V., Williams, J.M.G., and Teasdale, J.D. (2002) *Mindfulness-Based Cognitive Therapy for Depression*, Guilford Press, London.

5 Rogers, C.R. (1980) *Way of Being*, Houghton Mifflin, Boston.

10

Living Mindfully

Broadly speaking, we can distinguish two forms of mindfulness practice: formal and informal. Formal practices, such as the sitting meditations we've discussed, the body scan, yoga and so on, are key conditions in bringing about substantial inner change. As various studies have shown,[1] there is a clear link between the amount of time spent in engaging in these practices and beneficial changes in well-being. But informal practices have their place as well. These informal practices – mindfully eating, walking, washing the dishes, brushing your teeth and so on – do not, in and of themselves, bring about the sort of changes associated with formal practice.[1] But they do make for a richer inner life and considerable anecdotal evidence from people attending MBSR courses suggests

The Mindful Workplace: Developing Resilient Individuals and Resonant Organizations with MBSR, First Edition. M. Chaskalson.
© 2011 John Wiley & Sons, Ltd. Published 2011 by John Wiley & Sons, Ltd.

that there is a circular relationship between the formal and informal practices. People who regularly engage in formal mindfulness practice report that they find themselves more inclined to pay attention to – and to enjoy – many of the simple everyday tasks they engage in. And people who live their lives to the full in this way, noticing and enjoying their meals, the weather, other people and the world around them, also find themselves more readily able to engage in formal practice.

The range of possible informal practices is infinite. There is no limit to what you can pay attention to. But here is a list of possible practices[2] that you can engage in as the working day unfolds. You might try exploring a handful of these, using this list as a general guide to spark your own ideas – changing and adapting them according to your own circumstances and temperament.

- As you wake up, take a few moments to become aware of the world around you. The feel of the bedding, the quality of the light in the room, the sounds indoors and the sounds outside. Tune in to your breath and prepare yourself for whatever is coming next.
- If you drink a cup of tea or coffee first thing, make that an opportunity for mindfulness practice. Take a minute or two just for yourself. Enjoy the warmth of the cup or mug, the aroma of your drink and its flavour. Gaze out of the window and take in the sounds of nature or the city – most likely, the world is waking too.
- At the end of whatever formal practice you might do in the morning, take an extra moment or two to experience the results of the practice you've just done. Even if your mind didn't settle very easily, it's likely that you'll

now be more present and alert. Savour those feelings. Don't rush.

- If you walk to the bus, Tube or train station, make that a mindful walk. Perhaps take the chance to turn off your phone and any other communication device and give yourself over to enjoying those moments. Feel your feet on the ground and the movement in your legs and hips. Notice how you're breathing. Allow the range of your attention to broaden and expand – take in the world around you in this moment. And if you find that your mind wanders off into the past or future, if you start to become preoccupied with the tasks ahead, remind yourself that you're allowed to take a few moments for yourself, to refresh and prepare your mind for the day to come, and bring your attention back to this moment – to the sensations, perhaps, where your feet meet the pavement and to the feelings in your legs and hips.

- If you drive to work, take a few moments when you first get into your car just to connect with your breath and your body. Get yourself ready to drive mindfully to work.

- As you're driving, check in from time to time and become aware of any tension that may be there: your hands tensed at the wheel, shoulders hunched, stomach clenched. Breathe into those tensions, maybe letting them soften and move. Tensing up doesn't make you a better driver.

- Try choosing not to put on any music or not to listen to the car radio. Just be with yourself, your thoughts, feelings and body sensations as they change from moment to moment. And pay attention to the changing world outside your car. Stay in the moment and, when you find your mind wandering to the past or the future, just notice that and gently bring your attention back to the sensations of sitting there, driving.

- See what it's like to keep to the speed limit, or just below it. It might be more relaxing. If you're driving on a motorway, what's it like to keep to the slow lane?
- If you travel to work on a bus, Tube or train, maybe take a few moments on each journey just to tune in to yourself. Put aside the newspaper or your work, switch off your iPod and turn off your phone. Take some time now just for yourself. Follow your breath and settle inside yourself. These are rare moments, time just for you.
- If you park at your workplace, maybe make a point of parking further away from the entrance and give yourself the chance of a mindful walk in to work.
- If you're using public transport, maybe get off a stop earlier and do the same. The exercise has its own obvious benefits and it's another chance to tune in to yourself and establish some mindfulness. Enjoy your walk.
- However you got there, as you approach your office or other place of work, take a moment or two to orient yourself to the day ahead – how do you want to use this day?
- As you sit at your desk or workstation, take a few moments from time to time to tune in to your body sensations. Notice any tension that might be there and breathe into it – softening and easing.
- When you have a break at work, instead of reading the paper or searching on the Internet, take a real break. Get away from your computer – take a short walk and get outside if you can.
- At lunchtime, the same applies. Get away from your desk or workstation. If you can, turn off your phone and get some air. Pause. If you meet with colleagues over lunch, try talking about things other than work from time to time.

- Maybe eat one or two meals each week in silence. Maybe eat these meals more slowly than usual – enjoy the flavours and textures and just be with yourself.
- Find ways of setting up mindfulness cues in your workspace. Perhaps when your phone rings you could use that as an opportunity to come back to yourself. Maybe let it ring for a few more rings while you gather yourself before answering.
- Before heading home, review the day. Acknowledge what you've achieved, make a list of what you need to do tomorrow and – if you can – put your work down. Maybe you've done enough for now.
- Use your journey home as a way of making a transition. Walk or drive mindfully. Take your time.
- As you approach your front door, prepare yourself for home and get ready to enter a different mode of life.
- Maybe change your clothes soon after you get in and make a point of greeting everyone at home in turn. Look into their eyes and make a connection. Try taking 5 or 10 minutes to be quiet and still. If you live alone, feel what it is like to enter the quiet space of your own home, the feeling of coming into your own environment.

The ideas and practices here are just a guide and each of us will need to find our own ways to be mindful at work and mindful at home. But practising a few of these each day, making them part of your routine, can bring about significant changes to the texture and quality of each working day. Just a few minutes invested each day in that way, a few short and simple practices each day, can make for huge improvements in your overall quality of life. A life lived mindfully is so much richer and deeper.

References

1 Carmody, J., and Baer, R.A. (2008) Relationships between mindfulness practice and levels of mindfulness, medical and psychological symptoms and well-being in a Mindfulness-Based Stress Reduction program. *Journal of Behavioural Medicine*, 31, 23–33.
2 Santorelli, S.F. (1996) Mindfulness and mastery in the workplace, in *Engaged Buddhist Reader* (ed. A. Kotler), Parallax Press, Berkeley, pp. 39–45.

11

Putting on an Eight-Week Mindfulness Course in a Workplace Setting

In this chapter we will look at eight key questions to consider before putting on a workplace mindfulness course. After that, we will outline a typical workplace mindfulness course, bearing in mind that the specific shape and format of any course will be strongly influenced by the answers to the eight questions raised.

What Outcomes Are You Looking For?

Kabat-Zinn initially developed the eight-week mindfulness course to help people address issues of stress and chronic pain. As we've seen, the success of that programme gave rise to a host of similar interventions and we now find mindfulness courses targeted at a wide range of conditions with

The Mindful Workplace: Developing Resilient Individuals and Resonant Organizations with MBSR, First Edition. M. Chaskalson.
© 2011 John Wiley & Sons, Ltd. Published 2011 by John Wiley & Sons, Ltd.

positive results. Most of the research to date has focused on the various clinical applications of mindfulness but, in their 2010 systematic review of the neurobiological and clinical features of mindfulness meditations,[1] Chiesa and Serretti also examined the published research on the effects of mindfulness training on healthy subjects.

Mindfulness training, they found, led to a significant reduction in stress levels and MBSR significantly reduced many other measurable parameters, including those related to the potential for depression, anxiety and rumination. They found that it also enhanced interpersonal sensitivity, led to more adaptive coping strategies and increased self-compassion. But that is just a beginning, for they only had 11 published studies of the effects of mindfulness training on healthy populations at their disposal. Because the bulk of the research to date has investigated the relationship of mindfulness training to one or another mental or physical disorder, when considering the likely outcomes of the application of mindfulness in the workplace we need to extrapolate from these.

From what we currently know about the effects of mindfulness training, it is reasonable to believe that there will be significant beneficial impacts on a wide variety of workplace related issues. Extrapolating from published research, you might reasonably expect an eight-week MBSR course to deliver:

- a reduction in participants' levels of stress;
- an increase in their levels of emotional intelligence;
- increased interpersonal sensitivity;
- higher levels of personal resilience;
- lower rates of health-related absenteeism;
- increased self-awareness and awareness of others;
- enhanced communication skills;

- increased concentration and attention span;
- lower levels of impulsivity;
- a greater capacity to hold and manipulate information;
- improved sleeping patterns;
- lower levels of psychological distress, including depression and anxiety;
- higher levels of well-being and overall work and life satisfaction.

This list is far from exhaustive. No one, so far as I know, has yet researched the link between mindfulness and creativity or innovation, for example, and we've good reason to expect that there would be benefits there. Nor am I aware of any research into the impact of mindfulness on leadership where again there are strong reasons to expect positive outcomes.

The eight-week MBSR programme that was initially developed at the University of Massachusetts has been tweaked in a number of ways to address different issues and bring about different outcomes. According to Chiesa and Serreti's 2010 review,[1] mindfulness training has been shown to produce beneficial clinical and neurobiological effects in respect of the prevention of depression relapse, the reduction of overall depressive symptoms in major depressive disorder and the reduction of anxiety levels in bipolar disorder; it has been used to treat social phobia, alcohol and substance dependence and the psychological symptoms that accompany cancer. It has been used effectively to reduce blood pressure, chronic pain, the symptoms of rheumatoid arthritis, fibromyalgia, psoriasis, multiple sclerosis and HIV. It has also been used effectively to reduce stress.

Given this breadth of potential outcomes, each with its own particular approach, one of the first issues that anyone commissioning a workplace mindfulness intervention will need to address is: which of the many possible outcomes are they looking for? Is stress reduction the most important issue? Or resilience? Emotional intelligence? Communication skills? General well-being? Or some combination of all of these?

Some of the details of the way in which the course will be structured and delivered will depend on the answers to these questions. Courses can be tweaked to emphasize one or another issue. Broadly speaking, participants will learn a range of mindfulness skills and they will naturally come to apply these in whatever context they find themselves. But the instructor can choose to emphasize some applications more than others and he or she can add in materials appropriate to the outcome in question where appropriate.

Who Would the Course Be For?

Courses can be delivered to general staff, to middle managers, senior managers, senior executives, board members, or to any combination of these. Mixed groups have their advantages – it can be good for staff to see that people at all levels of an organization have their own issues to deal with and it can be a useful way to create links across an organization. In some workplaces, however, too much of a hierarchical span within a group can be inhibiting. Senior people might not want to exhibit their weaknesses and junior people might feel constrained by their presence. Some might be more comfortable in a group with people they don't know. Others may find it helpful to do the course as part of a workplace team. However the group is composed, the instructor will need to be sensitive to how these differences might play out and they should be discussed in advance with whoever is commissioning the course.

Will Attendance Be Voluntary or Not?

People's levels of engagement are likely to be higher with a course which they have voluntarily signed up for. Mindfulness *can* be delivered as part of a wider well-being initiative or a leadership-development programme which is not voluntary but, when one is asking people to undertake between 20 and 30 minutes of home practice a day for eight weeks, the issue of whether or not they volunteered for the course is important.

If attendance is *not* voluntary, and the eight-week course is being delivered as an aspect of a leadership development programme, for example, the instructor will need to make an extra effort to engage participants in the potential value of what they are doing and to enthuse them to engage in the various requirements of the course. Experience shows that an emphasis on the depth of the scientific research – especially the neuroscience research – that has so far been carried out with respect to mindfulness-based interventions can be an important part in bringing about participants' willingness to engage in the course. That, together with the quality of mindfulness they see embodied in their instructor, can be an important part of gaining their willingness to wholeheartedly participate.

How Will You Recruit Participants?

If courses are run on a voluntary basis, one method of recruitment is to offer a one-hour open taster session. Here, an instructor might detail some of the research around mindfulness and discuss its workplace applications. They might also run a few short meditation sessions – perhaps the raisin exercise, a five-minute mindfulness of breathing practice and the mindful minute. They should emphasize the need for home practice and for regular attendance at sessions. That will give potential participants a flavour of what they might expect and they could then be invited to sign up for a course. There is no recipe for the best method of recruitment, however, and it will be useful to experiment with alternatives.

Which Format Is Best Suited to the Client Group in Question?

MBSR and other mindfulness courses can be delivered in a wide variety of different ways to different workplace groups. Most typically, it can be delivered in much the way it was originally devised. Here, over eight sessions, it is taught by one or two instructors as an eight-week group-based process to groups of between 8 and 25 people, although none of that is fixed. Another option is to deliver the course over four half-days at fortnightly intervals. Here, one runs the first session, takes a tea or coffee break, and then runs the second session. A fortnight later one begins with the third session and, after a tea or coffee break, continues with the fourth session. And so on. The home-practice component is the same as for the usual eight-week course. Home practice for the first session is done after the first week and for the second session after the second week. The group meets again and home practice for the third session is done in the third week and for the fourth session the week after that. And so on.

It can be easier to manage the schedule of a four-session course (as opposed to an eight-session one) and participants sometimes find that the half-day format gives them more time to settle into the course each time and to leave their work problems behind. One potential disadvantage of a four-session course is that, over the fortnight gap between sessions, people can sometimes lose their motivation and home practice can suffer. A weekly check-in can make it easier to adhere to the home-practice requirement. For that reason it can be helpful to have participants pair up with a 'practice buddy' with whom they check in once a week – not to advise each other, but simply to discuss how they've got on with their home practice.

Courses can also be delivered one-to-one, as a form of personal coaching. And they can be delivered remotely, via telephone or video link. Such remote delivery can be made to a group or one-to-one. Group-based courses have lower per-capita costs and participants may also gain from sharing the experience of doing the course with others. One-to-one courses allow people more time to address their own particular issues. Senior people can feel more comfortable taking the course as a form of coaching and the flexible nature of one-to-one delivery might fit better with the complexity of their diaries. Remote delivery can be more cost-effective but it can feel a little more impersonal.

Where and When Is a Course Best Run?

Group-based courses can take place in the workplace or at a remote site. It can be organizationally simpler to deliver the course at the workplace – if there is a suitable, reasonably quiet and private meeting room available. The advantage of going offsite is that it can help people to leave work-related issues behind and an offsite environment can also be deliberately selected for quietness and other supporting factors.

To allow participants the time to change mode and focus fully on the requirements of the course, it's desirable that they leave the working day at their desk and change mode for the course. For that reason it may be best to run a course either in the first part of a working day or at the end of it. It's also possible to offer courses outside of working hours altogether.

How Much Time Can You Reasonably Ask Participants to Devote to Home Practice?

Courses delivered in health-care contexts typically require around 45 minutes of home practice a day for six days of each week that the course runs. In some workplaces, that may feel like too much to ask. We're not yet clear about the relationship between home-practice requirements and course outcomes. In 2008 Carmody and Baer[2] investigated this question by way of an eight-session group programme for individuals dealing with stress-related problems, illness, anxiety and chronic pain. The home-practice requirement for that course was 45 minutes per day. As is typical, they found that compliance to this requirement varied considerably and no one complied perfectly. But they did find that the time spent engaging in the home practice of formal meditation exercises was significantly related to the extent of improvement in most facets of mindfulness and in several measures of symptom reduction and well-being. The more one practised at home, the better the outcome.

That said, in the same year Klatt and colleagues[3] investigated the outcomes of a workplace MBSR intervention that only required 20 minutes of home practice a day. They found significant increases in levels of mindfulness, lower levels of perceived stress and improvements in quality of sleep. So the issue of exactly how much home practice will be needed is unresolved and the instructor will have to make a decision on what is best in conjunction with whoever commissions the course. For now, though, we can suggest that it will be somewhere between 20 and 45 minutes a day with the knowledge that compliance to that will be imperfect, whatever one finally decides.

Who Will Lead the Course?

Unlike some approaches that people working in organizational HR or Learning and Development will have encountered, it's not possible simply to read a book about MBSR or even attend an eight-week course for oneself and then go off and teach the approach to others. A large amount of what participants learn on such a course comes from their experience of mindfulness as embodied in their instructor. The open, allowing, kindly, curious, present-moment attention that the instructor brings to their interactions in the class is itself a significant part of the learning. Mindfulness can never be conveyed by a sequence of conceptual 'do this, do that' instructions, and the instructor's lived embodiment of mindful qualities is one of the most potent vehicles for communicating the 'felt sense' of these to course participants.

Participants bring deeply ingrained world views and schematic models with them on a course. We are used to thinking in terms of conceptual solutions to our problems and difficulties. For some issues, though, the mindfulness approach is highly counter-intuitive. Rather than seeking to 'fix' an anxious feeling, for example, an experienced instructor will try to help a participant to change their relationship to it. The participant might be gently guided towards an attitude of enquiry and investigation and helped to take a kind of affectionate interest in, for example, the physical manifestation of that feeling as it occurs. This needs to be done with great tact and skill and there is no simple recipe for doing it. The skills required for guidance such as this can only emerge from the instructor's lived application of them to their own experience over a number of years.

In setting out their guidance for teachers of Mindfulness-Based Cognitive Therapy, Segal and colleagues[4] suggest that prospective instructors have at least two years of personal mindfulness practice behind them before going on to deliver the course. That seems like a reasonable minimum. There are courses available in the United Kingdom for the training of MBSR instructors and these are detailed in Appendix 4, along with the 'Good Practice Guidance for Teaching Mindfulness-Based Courses' (Appendix 1), published by the UK Network of Mindfulness-Based Teacher Trainers.

An Eight-Week Course Outline

As we've seen, the eight-week mindfulness course can be adjusted in a number of ways. Here is the outline of the course that I have most experience in running. Based on the MBSR programme developed at the University of Massachusetts, it integrates within that some curriculum elements of the MBCT programme developed by Segal, Williams and Teasdale. This outline simply gives a taste of what an eight-week workplace course focused on stress reduction might look like. It presumes that participants will attend for two hours each session and that they do 45 minutes of home practice each day that the course runs. Both the session duration and the home-practice requirement can, as we've seen, be adjusted in various ways. It's also important to reiterate that the exact specifics of what is delivered will depend on which particular outcomes one is looking for.

Week 1 – Automatic pilot

The rationale for this session is that mindfulness begins when we recognize our tendency not to be mindful. We go about our days in a kind of 'automatic-pilot mode', doing what we know how to do without a great deal of awareness of ourselves, others and the world around us. In this session, participants come to see that fact to some extent. They also take the first steps towards some kind of commitment to learn how regularly to step out of automatic-pilot mode and become more aware.

Key themes for Session 1:
- introducing the course;
- building a supportive group environment for practice in this and future sessions;
- coming to understand the meaning of mindfulness;
- becoming aware of the significance of automatic pilot in our lives;
- noticing how bringing awareness to our experience changes the actual nature of the experience;
- seeing how problems can be worked with differently.

Main practices in Session 1:
- raisin exercise;
- body-scan meditation.

Other exercises in Session 1:

- introductions – 'What brought me to the course and what do I hope to get from it?'

Home practice for Session 1:
- body-scan meditation each day;
- doing one routine activity mindfully each day (the same activity each day);
- eating one meal mindfully at some point in the next seven days.

Week 2 – Dealing with barriers

The rationale of this week is that further focus on the body exposes more clearly the extent of chatter in the mind. Participants begin to see the extent to which their centre of attention tends to be located in their thinking processes. Sometimes we're more like balloons on sticks than people with bodies. Participants also come to see the way that mental chatter tends to control our reactions to everyday events. They see how we constantly interpret events, often wrongly, based on very limited information. They see how we have a tendency always to categorize our experience one way or another and how unused we are simply to describing bare sensations without categorizing them.

Key themes for Session 2:
- Coming home to the body and developing an awareness of the 'feeling tone' of different experiences.
- Working with difficulties in a new way and discovering new ways of learning.
- Discovering how we add layers to our experience and that it's often not situations themselves that cause us problems so much as our reactions to them.

- Seeing the nature of our perceptions – how we often misperceive and how these misperceptions can drive our behaviour.

Main practices in Session 2:
- body-scan meditation;
- mindfulness of breathing meditation.

Other exercises in Session 2:
- perception exercises to see how we often misperceive things because we're caught out by our assumptions;
- exercise to illustrate the way in which a situation plus an interpretation generate an emotion (and we often don't see that we've made an interpretation).

Home practice for Session 2:
- body-scan meditation each day;
- 10 minutes of mindfulness of breathing meditation each day;
- choosing a new routine activity to be mindful of each day;
- focusing on one pleasant event each day and completing a pleasant-events diary.

Week 3 – Mindfulness of the breath, and body in movement

In this week we learn more about the power of being present to our experience. Participants discover how they can work with difficulties, even intense difficulties, by maintaining a present-moment awareness. They may become even more aware of how scattered and unfocused their minds usually are. They also discover how intentionally working with their breath as a focus offers the opportunity to focus and gather themselves more effectively. They learn how bringing their attention deliberately to their bodies at times of difficulty can offer another perspective on the difficulty and can often instigate a more resourceful way of being with the difficulty.

Key themes for Session 3:
- further work on investigating the 'feeling tone' of experience;
- noticing again the layers that we add to our experience – especially difficult experience;
- learning how to deconstruct experience: coming to see how it is made up of thoughts, feelings and body sensations;
- deepening an understanding of the attitudinal qualities of mindfulness;
- learning more about the habitual and automatic patterns of our minds.

Main practices in Session 3:
- sitting meditation;
- mindful-movement practice – mindful stretching, yoga, qigong or some combination of these;
- mindful walking;
- three-step breathing space.

Other exercises in Session 3:
- enquiry into pleasant-events diaries.

Home practice for Session 3:
- mindful-movement sessions each day;
- 10 minutes of mindfulness of breathing each day;

- focusing on one unpleasant event each day and completing an unpleasant-events diary;
- practising the three-step breathing space three times a day.

Week 4 – Staying present

In this session we see the way in which our attempts to cling on to desirable experiences and push undesirable ones away colours our minds and drives our behaviour. We discover how this can scatter and fragment our attention, or narrow it too sharply. Instead, we now begin to learn a more mindful approach – learning to allow what is the case simply to be the case. We learn to take a wider view on our experience and to relate differently to it. We also learn about the neurophysiology of stress and begin to develop more resourceful ways of dealing with stressful situations. We learn more about how to use mindfulness skills to reduce reactivity.

Key themes for Session 4:
- exploring the nature of our experience – especially around attachment and aversion;
- developing the skills of deploying our awareness in different ways: broad and narrow focus;
- using mindfulness skills in stressful situations;
- learning to take a different perspective.

Main practices in Session 4:
- longer sitting meditation practice;
- three-step breathing space.

Other exercises in Session 4:
- unpleasant-events enquiry;
- exploring the territory of stress.

Home practice for Session 4:
- longer sitting meditation each day;
- mindful walking;
- three-step breathing space.

Week 5 – Acceptance: allowing/letting be

In this session we learn the value of allowing things to be just as they are without judging them or trying to make them different. This attitude of acceptance is a major part of taking care of ourselves and it allows us to see more clearly what, if anything, needs to change. Unless we can accept that what we are currently experiencing is simply what we are experiencing, and we *can* be with it, we have little choice in relation to it. Choice begins when we can accept – in an open and kindly way – that what is here now is simply what is here now. When we can do that, we may have some choice about what to do next.

Key themes for Session 5:
- seeing the way in which we habitually relate to our experience with clinging, with aversion or by 'tuning out';
- discerning the difference between reacting and responding;
- learning to allow what we feel simply to be what we feel;
- seeing how reactions play a key part in the experience of stress;
- developing an awareness of our reactions to difficulty and learning instead to respond to them.

Main practices in Session 5:
- sitting meditation: mindfulness of the breath, breath and body, sounds and thoughts, choiceness awareness;
- sitting with a difficulty in meditation;
- three-step breathing space.

Other exercises in Session 5:
- discussing Rumi's poem 'The guest house';
- experiential exploration of stress response and reactivity.

Home practice for Session 5:
- longer sitting meditation;
- become aware of moments of reaction; choose instead to respond;
- three-step breathing space, three times a day and as needed.

Week 6 – Thoughts are not facts

In this session the skills of reperceiving (see Chapter 1) are drawn out and made more explicit. Here we learn to see that thoughts are just thoughts and that, in the case of stress, catastrophizing thoughts can strongly colour the nature of our experience. We learn to see such thoughts for what they are – just thoughts – and to step back from them, without necessarily needing to question them or to seek alternatives. If such thoughts still have a strong pull on our awareness, we can choose to work with them more directly, with an attitude of investigation, curiosity and kindness.

Key themes for Session 6:
- the freedom that can come from realizing that thoughts are merely thoughts and that we don't have to act on them, engage with them or take them personally;
- developing a different relationship to thoughts and emotions, one of 'intimate detachment'.

Main practices in Session 6:
- full sitting meditation practice;
- breathing space – especially as a way of taking a wider view on thoughts.

Other exercises in Session 6:
- moods and thoughts exercise.

Home practice for Session 6:
- meditate for 40 minutes each day. Use the CD or not – as you wish;
- three-step breathing space, three times a day and as needed.

Week 7 – How can I best take care of myself?

In this session we explore the relationship between activities and stress. We each develop a 'map' of our own stress signatures, explore what we often do to accentuate that and what we can do to diminish stress. We begin to create strategies for recognizing and dealing with stress in the moment.

Key themes for Session 7:
- bringing awareness to our lives – the things we do that help us, the things that can get in our way and the behaviours that can be self-destructive.

Main practices in Session 7:
- longer sitting meditation.

Other exercises in Session 7:
- exercise to discover our own stress signatures;
- listing the activities that help and those that hinder when we are stressed;
- developing strategies to address stress in the moment;
- identifying what nurtures and what depletes us in the course of the day.

Home practice for Session 7:
- select, from all the formal meditation practices we've done, what you're going to use as your own practice on a regular basis in the future; begin to practise that;
- develop an action plan for dealing with stressors in the future;
- consider the shape of your day – what can you do to tweak things so that you experience more pleasure and mastery, and less of what depletes you.

Week 8 – Acceptance and change

The rationale of this session is that regular mindfulness practice can support a sustaining balance in life that makes for greater effectiveness and higher levels of satisfaction and well-being. The good intentions that have been generated on the course are now strengthened by linking the practices with positive reasons for taking better care of oneself.

Key themes for Session 8:
- this final session of the course is also the first session of the rest of your life;

- how to keep up the momentum and the discipline for both formal and informal practice;
- exploring a range of supports for future practice.

Main practices in Session 8:
- body scan.

Other exercises in Session 8:
- reviewing stress signatures and action plans;
- reviewing the course as a whole;
- questionnaires with personal reflections on the course;
- how to keep up momentum.

Home practice for Session 8:
- the rest of your life . . .

References

1 Chiesa, A., and Serretti, A. (2010) A systematic review of neuro-biological and clinical features of mindfulness meditations. *Psychological Medicine*, 40, 1239–1252.
2 Carmody, J., and Baer, R.A. (2008) Relationships between mind-fulness practice and levels of mindfulness, medical and psycho-logical symptoms and well-being in a Mindfulness-Based Stress Reduction program. *Journal of Behavioural Medicine*, 31, 23–33.
3 Klatt, M.D., Buckworth, J., and Malarkey, W.B. (2009) Effects of low-dose Mindfulness-Based Stress Reduction (MBSR-ld) on working adults. *Health Education & Behavior*, 36, 601–614.
4 Segal, Z.V., Williams, J.M.G., and Teasdale, J.D. (2002) *Mindfulness-Based Cognitive Therapy for Depression*, Guilford Press, London.

Appendix 1
Good Practice Guidance for Teaching Mindfulness-Based Courses

Published by the UK Network of Mindfulness-Based Teacher Trainers, January 2010.

A. Prior training or relevant background:
1. professional qualification in clinical practice, education or social context or equivalent life experience;
2. knowledge of the populations that the mindfulness-based approach will be delivered to, including experience of teaching, therapeutic or other care provision with groups and individuals;
3. a professional mental-health training that includes the use of evidenced based therapeutic approaches (if delivering MBCT).

The Mindful Workplace: Developing Resilient Individuals and Resonant Organizations with MBSR, First Edition. M. Chaskalson.
© 2011 John Wiley & Sons, Ltd. Published 2011 by John Wiley & Sons, Ltd.

B. Foundational training:
   1. familiarity through personal participation with the mindfulness-based course curriculum that you will be learning to teach;
   2. in-depth personal experience with daily mindfulness meditation practice, which includes the three core practices of mindfulness-based programmes – body scan, sitting meditation and mindful movement (plus any other core practice that is a necessary part of the programme being taught, e.g., the kindly-awareness practice in the Breathworks programme).
C. Mindfulness-based teacher training:
   1. completion of an in-depth, rigorous mindfulness-based teacher training programme or supervised pathway over a minimum duration of 12 months;
   2. development of awareness of the ethical framework within which you are working;
   3. development of awareness and recognition of the limitations and boundaries of your training and experience;
   4. engagement in a regular supervision process with (an) experienced mindfulness-based teacher(s) which includes:
      a. Opportunity to reflect on/enquire into personal process in relation to personal mindfulness practice and mindfulness-based teaching practice;
      b. Receiving periodic feedback on teaching from an experienced mindfulness-based teacher through video recordings, supervisor sitting in on teaching sessions or co-teaching and building in feedback sessions;
   5. participation in a residential teacher-led mindfulness meditation retreat.

D. Ongoing good-practice requirements:
1. ongoing commitment to a personal mindfulness practice through daily formal and informal practice and attendance on retreat;
2. ensuring that ongoing contacts with mindfulness-based colleagues are built and maintained as a means to share experiences and learn collaboratively;
3. ongoing and regular process of supervision by (an) experienced teacher(s) of mindfulness-based approaches which includes the areas cited in C4 above;
4. ongoing commitment to reflective practice supported by, for example, viewing recordings of own teaching sessions, connections with mindfulness teacher(s) and regular reading of books from the field of mindfulness;
5. engaging in further training to develop skills and understanding in delivering mindfulness-based approaches;
6. a commitment to keeping up to date with the current evidence base for mindfulness-based approaches;
7. ongoing adherence to the appropriate ethical framework of your background.

Appendix 2
Review of Significant Mindfulness Research

For a detailed list of peer-reviewed papers on current mindfulness research, see www.mindfulexperience.org. There are many hundreds of papers listed here. Below is a list of a few papers that pertain more particularly to mindfulness in the workplace:

Boyatzis, R., and McKee, A. (2005) In a bad spot? Try mindfulness, http://hbswk.hbs.edu/archive/5069.html (accessed 3 March 2011).

Boyce, B. (2009) Google searches, http://shambhalasun.com/index.php?option=com_content&task=view&id=3417&Itemid=244 (accessed 4 March 2011).

Chiesa, A., and Serretti, A. (2010) A systematic review of neurobiological and clinical features of mindfulness meditations. *Psychological Medicine*, 40, 1239–1252.

The Mindful Workplace: Developing Resilient Individuals and Resonant Organizations with MBSR, First Edition. M. Chaskalson.
© 2011 John Wiley & Sons, Ltd. Published 2011 by John Wiley & Sons, Ltd.

Chu, L.-C. (2010) The benefits of meditation vis-à-vis emotional intelligence, perceived stress and negative mental health. *Stress and Health*, 26, 169–180.

Davidson, R.J., Kabat-Zinn, J., Schumacher, J., *et al.* (2003) Alterations in brain and immune function produced by mindfulness meditation. *Psychosomatic Medicine*, 65, 564–570.

Fredrickson, B., and Branigan, C. (2005) Positive emotions broaden the scope of attention and thought-action repertoires. *Cognition and Emotion*, 19 (3), 313–332.

Friedman, R.S., and Forster, J. (2001) The effects of promotion and prevention cues on creativity. *Journal of Personality and Social Psychology*, 81 (6), 1001–1013.

Fryer, B. (2005) Are you working too hard? A conversation with Herbert Benson, http://hbr.org/2005/11/are-you-working-too-hard/ar/1 (accessed 2 March 2011).

Jha, A.P., Krompinger, J., and Baime, M.J. (2007) Mindfulness training modifies subsystems of attention. *Cognitive, Affective, & Behavioral Neuroscience*, 7 (2), 109–119.

Jha, A.P., and Stanley, E.A. (2010) Examining the protective effects of mindfulness training on working memory capacity and affective experience. *Emotion*, 10 (1), 54–64.

Lazar, S.W., Kerr, C.E., Wasserman, R.H., *et al.* (2005) Meditation experience is associated with increased cortical thickness. *Neuroreport*, 16 (17), 1893–1897.

Lutz, A., Greischar, L.L., Rawlings, N.B., *et al.* (2004) Long-term meditators self-induce high-amplitude gamma synchrony during mental practice. *Proceedings of the National Academy of Sciences*, 101 (46), 16 369–16 373.

McKee, A., Tilin, F., and Mason, D. (2009) Coaching from the inside: Building an internal group of emotionally intelligent coaches. *International Coaching Psychology Review*, 4 (1), 59–70.

Mental Health Foundation (2010) Mindfulness Report, London. Executive summary available from http://www.bemindful.co.uk/media/downloads/Executive%20Summary.pdf (accessed 28 February 2011).

Passmore, J., and Marianetti, O. (2007) The role of mindfulness in coaching. *The Coaching Psychologist*, 3 (3), 131–138.

Shapiro, S.L., Carlson, L.E., Astin, J.A., and Freedman, B. (2006) Mechanisms of mindfulness. *Journal of Clinical Psychology*, 62 (3), 373–386.

Silverthorne, S. (2010) Mindful leadership: When East meets West – Q&A with: William W. George, http://hbswk.hbs.edu/item/6482.html (accessed 7 March 2011).

Urry, H., Nitschke, J.B., Dolski, I., *et al.* (2004) Making a life worth living: The neural correlates of well-being. *Psychological Science*, 15 (6), 367–372.

Williams, K. (2006) Mindfulness-Based Stress Reduction (MBSR) in a Worksite Wellness program, in *Mindfulness-Based Treatment Approaches: Clinician's Guide to Evidence Base and Applications* (ed. R.A. Baer), Academic Press, Burlington, MA, pp. 361–376.

Appendix 3
Further Reading

Baer, R.A. (ed.) (2006) *Mindfulness-Based Treatment Approaches: Clinician's Guide to Evidence Base and Applications*, Academic Press, Burlington, MA.

Begley, S. (2007) *Train Your Mind, Change Your Brain: How a New Science Reveals Our Extraordinary Potential to Transform Ourselves*, Ballantine Books, New York.

Boyatzis, R., and McKee, A. (2005) *Resonant Leadership*, Harvard Business School Press, Boston.

Cherniss, C., and Goleman, D. (eds) (2001) *The Emotionally Intelligent Workplace*, Jossey-Bass, San Francisco.

Crane, R. (2008) *Mindfulness-Based Cognitive Therapy*, Routledge, London.

Germer, C.K. (2009) *The Mindful Path to Self-Compassion*, Guilford Press, London.

Germer, C.K., Siegel, R.D., and Fulton, P.R. (eds) (2005) *Mindfulness and Psychotherapy*, Guilford Press, London.

The Mindful Workplace: Developing Resilient Individuals and Resonant Organizations with MBSR, First Edition. M. Chaskalson.
© 2011 John Wiley & Sons, Ltd. Published 2011 by John Wiley & Sons, Ltd.

Gilbert, P. (2010) *The Compassionate Mind*, Constable, London.

Goleman, D. (1998) *Working with Emotional Intelligence*, Bantam Books, New York.

Hanson, R., and Mendius, R. (2009) *Buddha's Brain: The Practical Neuroscience of Happiness, Love and Wisdom*, New Harbinger Publications, Oakland, CA.

Hick, S.F., and Bien, T. (eds) (2008) *Mindfulness and the Therapeutic Relationship*, Guilford Press, London.

Kabat-Zinn, J. (1991) *Full Catastrophe Living: Using the Wisdom of Your Body and Mind to Face Stress, Pain and Illness*, Delta, New York.

Kabat-Zinn, J. (1994) *Wherever You Go, There You Are: Mindfulness Meditation in Everyday Life*, Hyperion, New York.

Kabat-Zinn, J. (2005) *Coming to Our Senses: Healing Ourselves and the World Through Mindfulness*, Piatkus Books, London.

McCown, D., Reibel, D.C., and Micozzi, M.S. (2010) *Teaching Mindfulness: A Practical Guide for Clinicians and Educators*, Springer-Verlag, New York.

McKee, A., Boyatzis, R., and Johnston, F. (2008) *Becoming a Resonant Leader*, Harvard Business School Press, Boston.

Segal, Z.V., Williams, J.M.G., and Teasdale, J.D. (2002) *Mindfulness-Based Cognitive Therapy for Depression: A New Approach to Preventing Relapse*, Guilford Press, London.

Siegel, D.J. (2007) *The Mindful Brain: Reflection and Attunement in the Cultivation of Well-Being*, W.W. Norton & Company, New York.

Smalley, S.L., and Winston, D. (2010) *Fully Present: The Science, Art and Practice of Mindfulness*, Da Capo Press, Philadelphia.

Williams, M., Teasdale, J., Segal, S., and Kabat-Zinn, J. (2007) *The Mindful Way through Depression: Freeing Yourself from Chronic Unhappiness*, Guilford Press, London.

Appendix 4
Further Training and Other Resources

There is a web site associated with this book, www.themindfulworkplace.com, which contains links and further information for those who want to explore further.

Anyone wishing to deliver mindfulness training in the workplace should first of all be trained themselves, both in mindfulness and in mindfulness instruction (see below). They should keep up their own practice and follow the 'Good Practice Guidance for Teaching Mindfulness-Based Courses' laid out in Appendix 1.

My associates and I are always happy to discuss prospects for workplace mindfulness training. A good place to start is with an email to info@themindfulworkplace.com.

Eight-week MBSR courses are now widely available throughout the world. Details of the public courses run by me

The Mindful Workplace: Developing Resilient Individuals and Resonant Organizations with MBSR, First Edition. M. Chaskalson.
© 2011 John Wiley & Sons, Ltd. Published 2011 by John Wiley & Sons, Ltd.

and my associates in the United Kingdom can be found at www.mbsr.co.uk and www.mindfulness-works.com. At present we run eight-week MBSR courses and the Mindfulness for Coaches course. We run Mindful Leadership courses on a bespoke basis and when there is the demand for it we will also run courses on teaching mindfulness in the workplace.

MBSR courses are available throughout the United Kingdom and the web site www.bemindful.co.uk is a good place to look for one local to you.

In the United States, the Center for Mindfulness in Medicine, Health Care, and Society is where it all started – see http://www.umassmed.edu/content.aspx?id=41252. They offer a range of programmes and their web site offers links to a host of local practitioners in the United States and elsewhere. As they note, however, they don't vouch for the quality of these.

Google may also help to locate a course for you if you search on MBSR. But beware – not everyone offering MBSR these days is qualified to do so. Check credentials carefully. If in doubt, phone the instructor and have a chat.

There are mindfulness teacher-training courses available in different parts of the world and a web search in your own location will be more up to date than this list could be.

The Centre for Mindfulness Research and Practice (part of the Department of Psychology at Bangor University) is where I trained myself and where I sometimes teach. They offer a master's degree in Mindfulness-Based Approaches and hold regular seven-day teacher-training retreats for those who have an established mindfulness practice. See www.bangor.ac.uk/mindfulness.

Index